LIVE BIG

Crossing the finish line
is just the beginning

LANCE CARTER

LIVE BIG
Crossing the finish line is just the beginning

Cover design by Dave Masuda
Cover photo by ©FinisherPix.com
Editing and interior layout by PacelliPublishing.com

Published by CreateSpace.com

ISBN-13: 978-1544278995
ISBN-10: 1544278993

Contents

Dedication

This book is dedicated to my biggest inspiration and the love of my life, Janine. Everything would be nothing without you, my love!

Thank you for always standing by me and believing in my dreams.

Foreword

by Kelsey Montgomery

Lance's dedication to his work and expansive heart were apparent the moment I met him.

I first saw him illuminated by a computer screen, sitting in the dark, as he woke up during a Seattle winter to have a 5 a.m. Skype call with me on the East coast. Lance structured my training workouts in preparation for the Lavaman Triathlon and remained an available resource for questions and guidance. From that point forward, his commitment to training and loads of inspirational stories kept me swimming, biking and running with vigor.

Lance has an acute attention to technical details. While visiting Seattle, I met Lance for a brief running workshop during which he critiqued the way I positioned my arms and paced my strides to improve overall efficiency. I ran from this meeting to my next destination and as I was arriving, a runner across the street traveling in the opposition direction yelled to me, "Great running form!" I couldn't believe my ears!

I was taught to compete with my head, learning proper athletic form and optimal structure of workouts. Additionally, I was taught to compete with my heart. On race day, he reminded those competing to dig deep and find the person or thing that lit the flame of inspiration within. He encouraged us to identify something for which we were grateful. With your heart, obstacles abate and lofty goals become achievable.

My journey from amateur to triathlete was largely fueled by efforts to remedy a broken heart following the death of my father. After time spent paralyzed by grief, I needed to rediscover movement. The process of moving my body gradually, but eventually, opened my heart and reignited my competitive spirit. My training evolved into a celebration of the body and ultimately, a celebration of life itself. What a wonderful gift to have a healthy body! Physical strength fostered a resilient mind.

Lance's words to commit with head and heart endured the peaks and valleys of the months leading up to the triathlon. The beauty of shared stories is in the practical knowledge gained, as well as the feeling of a heart energized. Lance's humble spirit will forever inspire as he shares his journey from novice to expert, navigating a series of challenging goals and repeatedly defying physical limitations.

The head and heart synchronized is an indisputable force!

Introduction

You may be asking the questions, "Is this it? Is this all there is? Is this all my life has to offer?" Perhaps you're feeling completely unmotivated and can't think of a single thing that inspires you to begin each day. Maybe you are content with your life but looking for that extra spark, something to take it to the next level. Maybe things are "fine," but fine is no longer good enough because you want excitement or a change in the status quo and you're ready for a challenge that will make you feel alive again.

What I've learned and what I want to share with you is how to energize your life through endurance sports such as triathlon, making life more fulfilling. More exciting. More alive. More inspired. It doesn't have to be triathlon. It can be any sport, activity or challenge that inspires you and pushes you outside of your comfort zone.

Training and racing provide countless opportunities to learn lessons that show up in all areas of your life. I can teach you how to move through and beyond self-doubt and create your own motivation. When you set off to accomplish something you never thought possible, it will challenge you on a variety of levels both physical and mental. More often than not, your greatest challenges lie mostly on the mental side. This holds true both for triathlon and other areas of your life as well.

Would you like to create more joy and happiness in your life? Would you like to be genuinely excited about tomorrow? Would you like to develop lifelong relationships that add meaning to your life? Would you like to increase your confidence and gain the courage to go after your dreams? If so, then you've found the right book - or maybe the right book has found you!

Like many young people, when I was twenty years old I was directionless and depressed. Staying in bed long past waking became a dark, yet comfortable friend which only affirmed that I was heading nowhere. I had no idea that in two short years I would complete my first IRONMAN® triathlon, which consists of a 2.4-mile swim, 112-mile bike, and 26.2-mile run. I had no idea that one race would completely alter the direction of my life. I would soon discover how that single decision would introduce me to an entirely new group of positive minded and supportive people that I now call dear friends. I would soon rid myself of an uninspired lifestyle, say goodbye to boredom, and wake up energized, looking forward to what my day had in store for me.

It's been more than twenty-three years since that first triathlon and I've been swimming, biking, running, stretching, strength training, and exercising ever since. Trust me, if I, an average everyday athlete with very little experience in swimming, biking, and running can complete nine IRONMAN triathlons, you too can give yourself a seemingly impossible challenge and elevate your life to a new level.

Even more importantly, as a coach for the last twenty years I've developed systems and strategies to help other people complete their races, challenge themselves, and grow as people, increasing their vitality along the way. The majority of people I've coached have been through Team In Training (TNT), a fundraising endurance program through The Leukemia and Lymphoma Society. Most "TNTers" are participating in their first endurance events. I've coached more than two thousand people and have observed that most adults default to the idea that they are incapable of achieving new milestones. I can see right through their self-imposed obstacles while empowering them to move through and beyond their limitations so they can grow as athletes, and more importantly, as people. It is amazing when, with the right encouragement, they can see what I see–potential. We are all capable of so much more than we allow ourselves to believe.

I use the sport of triathlon as an example of possibilities and coach athletes on how to apply training and racing lessons to other parts of their lives so they can soar to new heights. Herein lies the reason I've written this book; the source of inspiration which keeps me coaching year after year. People are indeed capable of more than they think and often they simply need just one person to strongly believe in them until they believe in themselves. The moment they begin to believe in themselves is when magical transformation begins.

I'm thrilled this book has found its way to you and you are reading it. I'm convinced you can add more vitality to your life, a greater sense of purpose, and a deeper desire to LIVE more fully. You absolutely are capable of more in your life. Don't wait for life to come to you. Read this book and use the strategies to break through your self-imposed barriers. Choose to take your life to the next level.

Let me ask you a question. Do you want a life full of tomorrows that repeat the same old pattern? Or do you want a life full of tomorrows that inspire you? Let's do this!

1

What Else?

People are not lazy. They simply have impotent goals – that is goals that do not inspire them.

Tony Robbins

The First Day of the Rest of My Life

1993. July 31. Santa Rosa, California. 103 degrees.
Roughly 2:30 pm.

I rack my bike and attempt to run. With every step, it feels like someone is beating the front of my legs with a baseball bat, so I walk. Always the optimist, I attempt to run about every half-mile only to experience the same excruciating pain. I want to quit because I want the pain to end. I want to continue so I can prove to myself that I have the inner strength NOT to quit. For the next six hours of a nearly fourteen-hour day of exercise, the Angel and Devil in my mind play mental ping pong.

This is my most poignant memory from that scorching hot day back in 1993. It was also the first time I had ever swam 2.4 miles or biked 112 miles, let alone do them back to back in the same day and attempt to run afterwards.

It was exhausting, not only physically, but mentally. However, the experience of pushing through the pain to finish was unexpectedly liberating. Crossing the finish line was the beginning of a new me. I had no idea how that day would completely alter the course of my life.

From Depressed to Inspired

Let's go back to 1990 to when I was twenty years old. Not unlike many twenty-somethings, I felt lost. I wasn't quite sure what I wanted to do with my life. I was attending classes at California State University, Chico, though to be honest, I felt like I was wasting my time. I had no direction and no clear motivation to finish my degree, as it seemed to hold no future purpose for me. I was depressed, sleeping more than ten hours each night. I was unmotivated and my days were filled with very little joy. This continued for nearly two years. Eventually I grew tired of being tired. I desperately wanted my life to be different. To be better. To be *more*. I just had no idea how to change my circumstances.

One day, around my twenty-second birthday I was wandering through the self-help section at the local book store when I picked up a copy of Tony Robbins' book, *Unlimited Power*. In many ways, I felt like the book picked me. I had never heard of Tony Robbins. I looked at several book covers that day, occasionally reading the book jackets; for some reason that book spoke to me. I'm grateful it did because that book helped me change my life.

So much of what I read in that book rocked my world in a remarkable way. One of the many ideas I read was that to create massive motivation and inspiration you must choose a massive goal. I remember reading that if you felt depressed you needed a bigger goal, something that almost seemed impossible. Something so motivating it would get you out of bed in the morning, excited for the day. Oh, how I'd welcome that feeling!

When I read, "People are not lazy. They simply have impotent goals – that is goals that do not inspire them," I felt the heaviness lift from my shoulders. It was a light bulb moment for me because I realized I had nothing in my life that was inspiring to me, nothing that was motivating me. I was just moving through life day after day with zero ambition. Instantly I realized I wasn't "fundamentally flawed" as I had come to believe. I simply needed a larger-than-life goal that would inspire and motivate me. From that point on I was on the lookout for an idea that would light a fire within me. The rest was fate.

As a college student completely on my own financially, I had a job as a bus boy at Tres Hombres in Chico, California. One day in November of 1992, a couple of months after reading Robbins' idea about inspired goals, I was getting ready for work and I turned on the TV to listen and half-watch some sports. I turned the channel to ABC where college football just ended and it was followed by an event I had never heard of. I checked CBS and NBC. There were no sports on either of the other two channels, so I went back to ABC. At least it was a type of sports, even though I had never heard about this thing called "triathlon."

I watched the triathlon coverage, and from what I could gather these athletes who were now riding their bikes 112 miles on "The Queen K Highway" through the "extreme heat caused by the Hawaiian lava fields" had already swam 2.4 miles in the ocean. I was half paying attention, mostly listening and occasionally watching. I heard the announcers say they would soon be running a marathon and now I was more interested because I understood what a marathon was. Even though I had never run a marathon, I knew several people who had and knew enough to know that running a marathon was difficult. The fact they would be running a marathon *after* swimming and biking . . . crazy!

Over the next hour I became captivated. I remember it so vividly because I was never late to my job and I was going to be late if I kept watching. I had about a ten-minute commute by bike to Tres Hombres. I was totally engrossed and it was scheduled to end at 5 p.m. which was when I was due at work. I needed to turn off the TV, hop on my bike and get my butt to work. However, I simply could not pull myself away.

I was mesmerized and it felt like my feet were glued to the floor. These people were doing something so incredibly epic I thought it seemed impossible for an ordinary human being (like me). I watched to the very end, listening intently to the announcer talk about these people trying desperately to beat the midnight deadline for something called IRONMAN World Championship in some town named Kailua-Kona on the Big Island of Hawaii. Something deep inside me stirred. Even now, recalling this story I feel that same stirring deep inside.

Finally, at 4:55 p.m. when the credits began to roll, I jetted out the door, hopped on my bike and pedaled as hard as I could. My manager Joe was waiting for me, wanting to know why I was late. The fact that I was sweating profusely from riding so hard helped sell my story that I got a flat tire. *(Sorry I lied to you Joe.)* Clearly, I had made an effort to get to work on time and lucky for me it was the only time I was late.

All night at work I had a hard time concentrating on my tasks as all I could think about was this crazy and seemingly impossible thing called IRONMAN. I still did not entirely understand what it was, but before my shift ended, I had decided that completing IRONMAN World Championship in Hawaii would be my goal. That was the thing I would do to spark massive action. The inspirational goal Tony Robbins promised would pull me out of my funk. I committed myself to the fact that one day I would do it. KONA became my mantra.

VINEMAN®

The next day I went to Fleet Feet Sports to find out what exactly this thing was that I had committed to doing. Something so epic it would change my life simply by its impossible nature. I picked up a copy of *Triathlete Magazine* that had some guy named Mark Allen on the cover with blood soaked through his shoes. I read every article. I was hooked. 2.4-mile swim. 112-mile bike. 26.2-mile run. That's insane, I thought. Sure, why not? What do I have to lose?

Although IRONMAN sounded impossible, I realized that other "super-human" people had done it, proving it was indeed possible. Maybe I could do it too. Perhaps I should do one before I go to Hawaii. How would I even get into this race in Hawaii? So many questions.

Triathlete Magazine had an ad for a race in Santa Rosa called VINEMAN which was only thirty minutes from where I had grown up in Calistoga, California and just a three-hour drive from Chico. VINEMAN was the same distance as the one I'd seen on TV. In fact, at that point, I thought the full distance was the only distance available for the sport of triathlon.

How perfect, I thought. I could stay at my parents' house which would save money on lodging, and I didn't have to fly to get there. As you can imagine, a bus boy in college with no car did not have much in the way of disposable income. *Ah, to be young again!* I decided I would do VINEMAN on July 31, 1993. After all that was a full eight months away; plenty of time, right?

Great! Now what? Where would I begin? As fate would have it the Chico State Physical Education department had a course called Triathlon 101 that began in January. Excellent! I could sign up for the class and be good to go. Everything seemed to be magically coming together.

Never mind that I could barely swim twenty-five yards. Never mind that I only owned a mountain bike, mainly as way to get to classes and work; a whopping three miles each way. I think the most I'd ever ridden was five miles. Never mind that my idea of running was to jog two miles to stay in shape for basketball. Looking back now, it's clear that ignorance is bliss. Knowing now what I didn't know then . . . what the hell was I thinking?

The night before the race I met up with a couple of my closest friends for dinner and every one of them told me there was no way I would finish. It was not that they didn't believe in me, but they simply didn't think it was humanly possible. I remember the dialog like it was yesterday, "You mean to tell us this has already been done? People actually do this? In one day? That's crazy. Dude, that's like swimming from here to town (Calistoga). That's like riding your bike from here to Chico. That's like running from Calistoga to Napa. There's no way. Not possible." I too had serious doubts whether I would be able to pull this off, but I was determined to find out. All I could think was, "What have I gotten myself into?"

Why is it that our brains are so good at self-sabotage? Why is it that our brains can list with lightning speed all the reasons we will fail, and all the reasons we should give up before we even begin? We can list our inadequacies and shortcomings at the drop of a hat but when it comes to listing even a few reasons we will succeed, it takes effort. Therein lies the struggle every one of us faces - the inner battle to overcome our self-doubt which keeps us from trying.

My twenty years of coaching and self-discovery have helped me learn a myriad of techniques I've used on myself as well as the athletes I've coached. Often we need to quiet our brains with meditation, journaling or list building to allow our brains to come up with a few positive things to support us. Until we've conditioned ourselves to think positively through practice, the brain automatically goes to the negative. Even when we've developed a habit of thinking positive we still have to resist the urge to return to the dark side. Later in the book, I will share with you many of the techniques and exercises that have proved the most effective for me as an athlete and coach.

As I listened to my friends express their doubts about my finishing IRONMAN, the only positive thought I could muster was, "It's possible because some people have already done it." Every other thought was condemning. "Was I ready? Could I do this? Was I putting my health at risk? What if they were right and I failed; was I a failure? Would it be better for me to simply not race? Could I create a plausible excuse and save face?" I decided I would rather know I tried and failed than be haunted by the lifelong wondering and "what-ifs."

Leading up to the race I had only swum a maximum of one hour in the pool, biked ninety miles *once*, which I completely bonked (the cycling term for running out of energy) at mile 80, not knowing to eat while cycling. I think sixteen miles was my longest run, possibly shorter.

I had no idea how to prepare or even the faintest idea of how much to train. My Physical Education course, *Triathlon 101*, shed light on the fact most triathlons were actually quite short in comparison to a full distance triathlon. The PE course taught the basics of how to train for a "normal" triathlon which was the "International Distance Triathlon" now more commonly referred to as an Olympic Distance Triathlon (1500-meter swim, 40-

kilometer bike, 10-kilometer run). During *Triathlon 101* it began to dawn on me that I unknowingly committed to something far beyond my capability. I was too embarrassed and afraid to tell the instructor I was signed up for IRONMAN. I'd just have to roll the dice.

The day of the race I lost fifteen pounds due to dehydration. At one point on the run an ambulance was following me and pulled up alongside and asked if I was okay, probably because I looked like death. I knew it was hot and had heard a volunteer say it was over 100 degrees and "115 on the pavement." I wasn't sure what "115 on the pavement" meant except that my feet sure did feel hot! I remember around mile 18 of the marathon feeling like I desperately needed to pee, stepping into a port-a-potty that felt like a sauna, and only producing a few drops of brown liquid. What on earth was this? I had absolutely no idea what that meant. What was happening to my body? Whatever it meant, I was pretty sure it was not good.

This point in the race coincided with the location on the run course when I saw the ambulance. I would only find out much later brown urine was a sign of severe dehydration. I had a feeling the ambulance driver knew something I didn't, but I also didn't want to ask. I was afraid he'd tell me I was done and I would be removed from the race, never having the chance to cross the finish line.

During this death march, I could see holograms of an angel on one shoulder and a devil played by Darth

Vader on the other. I find it comical that the devil was played by Darth Vader and I remember laughing during the race about it. Why wasn't the angel portrayed by Princess Leia? At any rate, the two were constantly going back and forth with Darth Vader telling me to drop out and the angel telling me to keep going. This went on for hours. It was very surreal and very powerful. The "run" if I can call it that took six hours. To this day, I still get goosebumps telling this story.

Eventually I made it to mile marker 25 and for the first time all day I thought I just might finish. After another half mile, as I took a left turn into the business park near the Sonoma County Airport, I saw the bright green grass and people cheering. Then all of a sudden, my friends spotted me and Trent came sprinting towards me, screaming like a mad man, telling me what a "f***ing stud" I was, pumping me up for the last half mile. These were the same friends who less than twenty-four hours earlier had questioned if I could do this race, so you can imagine their shock and excitement. As I ran down the finish chute I could see my mom and Nana who were there to cheer me on as well. Ten seconds after crossing the finish line Corey handed me a beer, of which I promptly took a big celebratory swig. Hey, what do you expect from 23-year-olds?

From a Day to a Career

In the days and weeks which followed, I noticed I seemed to be walking around with a permanent grin on my face.

People commented that something about me seemed different. I was simply amazed at what I had just accomplished. I had completely shattered my beliefs about what I was capable of and I began asking myself a profound question; one that would forever change the course of my life.

"If I can do IRONMAN, what else could I do?"

By finishing that race when virtually every person I knew thought it was impossible, and I wasn't sure if I could finish, my self-confidence began to grow stronger each time I recalled crossing the finish line. I found I loved the training far more than I ever would have imagined. I also found myself spending more and more time in Fleet Feet Sports, the running store in Chico. I'd often just pop in to look at all the shoes and check out the swim gear. I was the proverbial kid in a candy store. When I was inside Fleet Feet it just felt comfortable; it felt like home and it made me happy. It wasn't long before I began to dream of one day owning my own running store.

Prior to finishing my first full distance triathlon I had no grand dream about what I would do for a career. I did not have a desire to work in any particular field; though I knew teaching was a strength of mine. My most likely path seemed to be teaching high school physical education and coaching basketball. What bothered me most about pursuing that path was my perception of teaching as a thankless job. Growing up I heard so much complaining about teachers from parents and it seemed the teachers were not truly happy, often complaining about the school administration and the parents. It seemed like a circular firing squad of blame, not to mention being a high school teacher was and still is one of the lowest paying careers. It's sad to see our teachers of today taking part-time jobs to make ends meet.

Deep down I wanted to find a career that would ignite my passion for life, make me financially successful, and not work myself to the bone or destroy my soul. Growing up, many people I knew complained about their jobs and it just seemed like a crappy way to live. But what was the alternative?

I'm not entirely sure why, but I believed that a fantastically successful career while doing something I loved was for "other" people and not me. I believed I was destined to be another cog in the wheel; another person heading off to work doing the same thing for forty years waiting to retire while I bitched and complained. I knew enough to realize that wasn't who I wanted to be or who I was at my core. I wanted more but I didn't know how to go about getting it. Doing IRONMAN gave me the confidence to dream bigger. "Maybe I can make a career within the sport of triathlon somehow," I thought to myself.

Accomplishing that first epic full distance triathlon also taught me another valuable lesson – the value of proper preparation. This time, instead of jumping right in and opening my own running store I thought I should go to work in a running store and treat it as an apprenticeship so I would understand what owning a store really meant. I needed an education in operating a running store.

In 1994 when my then girlfriend and now wife of twenty years, Janine and I moved to Seattle, I got a job at Super Jock 'n Jill, a running store located in Green Lake. I had no idea that Green Lake was the epicenter of Seattle's running scene or that Super Jock 'n Jill was one of the top running stores in the nation. As I came to understand these facts I took it as a sign that I was on the right track. From day one I was on a mission to learn everything I could about operating a running store so when it was my time I would be ready. Little did I know it would be ten years before I opened my own running store in partnership with two colleagues.

Triathlons teach us so many valuable lessons. For example, determination is critical, both for endurance sports and in life. The one characteristic that got me through VINEMAN was not giving in to the desire to quit. Determination was also the key factor that allowed me to keep working at it until my two friends and I could finally open our very own running store named Everyday Athlete in Kirkland, Washington.

It would have been easy to give up this dream. It was going to take too much money. The perfect location wasn't available. It might not succeed. It's astounding how many reasons the human mind can come up with in order to derail our dreams and goals. It takes a lot of strength and fortitude to press on when the desire to give up is so strong and seems so easy. Triathlons in many ways are microcosms of life.

The biggest lesson I learned from my first IRONMAN triathlon, which has continually been reinforced in my own life and with the athletes I've coached, is that we are all capable of achieving, doing, and being so much more when we allow ourselves to believe.

2

Positive Thinking and Uncovering My Purpose

Things turn out best for the people who make the best of the way things turn out.

John Wooden

LIVE BIG

Time for Change

There comes a period in everyone's life when it's simply time for a change. The challenging part is (1) recognizing it and (2) doing something about it. Too often we know we need to make a change for months and often years before we actually gather the courage to act. Some experts would say we simply need enough pain to build up before we become motivated to do something about it.

There's the saying, "Whenever a door closes another one opens." Instead I like to say, "When a door closes, a window opens, then you need the courage to jump out and the faith that either a parachute will open or you'll grow wings and fly." When a door closes, it is typically not the case that a new beautiful door to a better existence magically appears. Instead the real world is much scarier and the thought of starting from scratch can be terrifying, or even paralyzing.

Death by a Thousand Negative Thoughts

The running store my partners and I opened in 2004 was humming along nicely with double digit growth for five years. We were quite pleased with life. Everything was working out just as we expected. Then in 2009 the Great Recession got its fangs into our business just as it did the rest of the country. Suddenly, things were not so easy, and the joy of owning a running store slowly turned into a struggle.

"Flat was the new up." That's what our vendor reps were telling us. Geez, I hate that saying. Business continued to be "flat" for the next four years, up one percent one year, down one percent the next. The years of 2009 and 2010 were the, "Let's see what happens years." We figured we could simply ride it out, however the depressed economy drug on for much longer than we expected. Midway through 2011, one of the three original owners left the business making it a little easier to meet the expenses with a third less payroll.

Then in 2012, from January through September, business was the best it had ever been. All we could think was, "Finally the recession is over." Things were once again looking up. Unexpectedly, October brought with it a sharp reduction in sales from the previous year. The next twelve months showed the same pattern. Sales were down consistently and it was alarming to say the least. Sales continued to decline year after year, while rent, utilities, freight and other expenses continued to rise.

It was clear the online retail world was seriously and negatively impacting traditional "brick and mortar" stores like ours. I spent the next twelve months hoping the downward trend would stop. It didn't. In November of 2013 I brought in several business consultants for advice. The conclusions were all the same: Everyday Athlete simply could not afford to support two owners. There were no more expenses left to cut; one of us would have to go.

I decided in April of 2014 to do something I never thought I would do; hire a life coach. I was struggling with whether to ignore the advice of the business consultants or forge a new path and become a full-time triathlon coach. There was much fear and worry on my part, wondering if I could make a living as a triathlon coach, not to mention the fear of starting over.

A few friends of mine, Christie and Theresa, were raving about a life coach named SheAh Prince Eternal, who specialized in the Law of Attraction. The Wikipedia definition of the Law of Attraction is, "the name given to the maxim. 'like attracts like.' which in New Thought philosophy sums up the idea that by focusing on positive or negative thoughts a person brings positive or negative experiences into their life. This belief is based upon the idea that people and their thoughts are both made from 'pure energy' and the belief that like energy attracts like energy."

I had no idea my mind had become a toxic wasteland of negative thought. Where had the positive, "I did IRONMAN, I can do anything" guy go? I guess several years of grinding away, struggling in business, not knowing how we would make payroll or pay the rent wore away like water slowly eroding rock, gradually but continuously, until the landscape no longer resembled anything it once did.

Constantly walking around thinking negative thoughts SUCKS! Yet so many of us do exactly this. You may even find yourself in a similar situation right now.

After several months of doing a lot work on myself I am extremely passionate about telling you it is absolutely possible to change your thinking. I can't even believe how different my brain is operating now, roughly a year and a half later. Yes, it took me several months to begin the shift and over a year to come to a point where my thinking was the opposite of what it had been. If you were hoping I was going to tell you it can happen overnight, no luck. You won't hear that from me. I'm not saying it's not possible; it just didn't happen that way for me. I had to work at it but I wouldn't change my experience for the world because I am so much stronger having gone through the struggle.

The transformation I've undergone is one of the best gifts life has ever given me. I am so grateful each day. Living with my reclaimed positive mental state is such a joy, especially when I think about the past several years that preceded this past year. Best of all, I can share the lessons I've learned with other people and help them experience a higher quality of life. You're probably wondering how I did it. Keep reading!

Positive Journaling

The biggest realization that I had when I began the work with SheAh was how negative my mindset had become. I didn't consider myself a negative person at all. Yet there I was trapped in a state of worry and anxiety, constantly thinking of all the bad things that were going to happen to Everyday Athlete and by extension, to my life, which included the thought of going out of business, bankruptcy, and being a complete failure.

At the request of my coach, I began spending a few minutes each day writing in a journal. I didn't write anything specific, just what was rattling around in my brain. After a couple of months, I reviewed what I had been writing and was shocked. Nearly all of what I was writing was either negative or neutral at best. I wasn't thinking positive thoughts. At all!

I decided that from then on, I would stop journaling and start "positive journaling." Clearly, I needed to turn things around. One day I came up with an idea for an exercise. I challenged myself to write down ten positive things about myself. I was shocked to find that I wrote only a couple of things down before continuing became a real struggle.

Want to give it a try? Take out some paper or a journal and write down ten positive things about yourself. What comes up for you? It's not just what you write down but what comes up internally for you. Do you notice there may be something you want to write only to have your internal dialog question its validity? Maybe it was easy for you and you breezed through it. If so, congratulations! I've given this exercise to many people and have found most people struggle with it just as I did.

I was able to write down three things before I hit the wall, to put it in terms of a marathon, where hitting the wall occurs around mile 20. It was obvious I needed to overcome this roadblock. I decided to write ten statements about myself, allowing them to be anything from positive to negative. I wrote the first ten things that came to mind. I already had the three positive statements, so I wrote the next seven.

Perhaps even more shocking to me was how quickly I filled the page with seven negative things about myself. While I had to think, ponder, and even question my three positive statements, my pen couldn't keep up with my brain when it came to writing down negative statements. I remember thinking, "That's seriously messed up!" I felt a great sadness for myself along with a great deal of disappointment.

Each day for the next couple of months I wrote down the same ten statements and then I worked on rewriting them; replacing the one before it when I was ready to move forward. Each time I strengthened them, making them more positive. While doing this I came up with the term, "Bridge Statements." Bridge Statements are positive statements that resonate as sincere and are stepping stones to bigger, bolder positive statements.

Bridge Statements

Each statement was a bridge allowing me to move from one statement to the next, consistently getting more positive with each new statement. I had guidelines for myself. I would repeat a particular statement for several days until I felt congruency; alignment of my mind and body. When I was ready to move forward I would create a new statement that was more positive and it had to meet my criteria of feeling genuine.

Any time I tried to write down a statement that was too great a leap I would experience a sickening pit feeling in my stomach and I would feel like a fraud. When I went further than my mind and body was ready to go, or when a statement did not feel authentic, it only made me feel worse. I knew I'd need to go slowly and at my own pace, no matter how long it took.

Here's an example of how I used Bridge Statements when it came to how I thought of myself as a coach. Despite a great many people telling me I was an excellent coach, I did not feel like an excellent coach or believe I was an excellent coach. I went slowly in my transformation. At first, I would only allow myself to write down, "I am a pretty good coach." Eventually I hoped to not only write down, but genuinely feel that I was an excellent coach. Over a couple of months, I would receive praise from athletes I coached and they would tell me what a great coach I was or share with me a fantastic result they experienced due to my coaching.

Eventually I allowed myself to accept these compliments. Accepting praise is something I've never been good at and recently learned that I am, or rather *was*, someone who deflected praise and compliments. For example, one Bridge Statement I repeated for a couple of weeks was, "Marian told me that I am an excellent coach." This is something that was true. Marian did tell me that. I also know her well enough and trust her enough to know that she would never tell me something if she did not sincerely mean it. It allowed me to accept the idea that at least one person felt this way about me and maybe I could allow myself to feel the same way. As I did that, an amazing thing happened. I began to allow myself to accept more compliments from athletes I coached. More importantly, I began to feel more confident in my coaching abilities.

I still remember the moment I wrote down, "I am an excellent coach." I hadn't planned on writing that statement. It wasn't premeditated; it just came out. I sat at my dining room table and marveled at the transformation I had gone through; right before my very eyes without even realizing it. Over the course of a couple of months, I was now thinking completely differently. Amazing!

Here is the progression of how I strengthened my Bridge Statements regarding how I felt about myself as a coach: *I am an okay coach. . . . I am a pretty good coach. . . . Marian thinks I am a great coach. . . . I just received two separate emails praising my coaching; perhaps I am a better coach than I give myself credit for . . . . You know what? I am a good coach. . . . I've got lots of experience and I've helped many people. . . . I care about my athletes and I'm always looking for ways that I can improve as a coach, which makes me a very good coach . . . . **I'm a great coach!**

As you can see, each statement builds on the one before it. I would only write down the statement which felt true to me and I would spend the amount of time needed at each step. When I was ready to move forward I would then work towards the next Bridge Statement.

Of course, you can and should create your own Bridge Statements. Give it a try! Pick an area of your life that you want to improve your mindset. Just remember to keep your statements positive and to keep building them to be increasingly more positive as you move toward your end goal. Make each new statement just enough of a stretch that you can believe it, but it still pushes your comfort zone. Write down your statement each day and you'll know when you are ready to move on because you'll notice you feel different. Identify where you are beginning and where you want to end up. You only need to move one step at a time. Just think of one statement that is more positive than your starting point. The rest of the steps will come to you when you are ready and before you know it you'll blurt out your goal statement.

Here's an example I used with an athlete I coached who was just learning to swim. She constantly talked about what a poor swimmer she was. I had her replace every negative statement regarding her swimming with the following Bridge Statement, "I am becoming a better swimmer." That one subtle shift led her from an inability to swim twenty-five yards to, three months later, finishing her first Sprint Distance Triathlon which included a half-mile open water swim!

If she had continued to remind herself how bad she was at swimming, it's very likely she would have given up before the race. It was easier for her to show up to coached swim sessions when she reminded herself that she was improving. With improvement, there is hope and with hope there is reason to continue. What if she allowed her brain to be stuck on that thought - that she would not be able to complete the swim? It certainly would have made it easier for her to throw in the towel and give up on the goal of completing her first triathlon. Leading up to the race we did an open water swim and covered about an eighth of a mile. The next time we covered about a quarter of a mile. With each successive open water swim she gained more confidence and her thoughts shifted from, "I can't do this" to, "Maybe I can do this," to "I can totally do this." This was all made possible by how she reframed her swimming ability.

Replace "Have to" with "Get to"

You can completely change your mindset with one tiny shift in your language. Ever notice how often people use the term, "have to?"

"I have to go to work."
"I have to exercise."
"I have to go visit my family."
"I have to go watch my kid's soccer game."
"I have to meet my friends for dinner."

How do *you* use this phrase? Do you use it often? If you are like me, you are not even aware how frequently you say it. For most of my life I would say, "I have to go work out tomorrow," or some version of it. A few years back I was in physical therapy for several months treating an injury that prevented me from exercising. I realized exercising was a privilege and not a God-given right or even a chore, as the phrase "have to" implies. I realized I "get to" exercise. Exercise is a gift to me and one of the key components of my life and my daily happiness. I'm sure my wife and friends were sick and tired of hearing me complain about how I couldn't exercise during that time. I know I was much grumpier and less patient with people, probably even a jerk on occasion. I was treating something so sacred with disdain by saying, "I have to exercise today."

Think for a moment about what "have to" implies. It implies you don't have a choice. It implies it's something that you don't want to do and/or dread doing. As soon as you use the phrase "I have to" you are setting yourself up to be in a state of negativity. Simply using the phrase implies there is something else you'd rather be doing. How can you be in state of positivity when you'd rather be doing something else?

One of the easiest ways to understand this is to think about the thing you "have to" do and imagine that thing is instantly and completely taken away from you. Go ahead, complain about your job. Complaining about work is one of the most common gripes. Now imagine you are transported back in time, only a few years, to the Great Recession. Now imagine you lose your job and go several years before getting another job, and to top it off the new job pays significantly less than your current job. This was a very real and far too common occurrence for many people in 2008. All of a sudden, your current job looks better and you might see that you "get to" go to work.

Begin to notice any time you or your friends use the words "have to" and take a moment to examine the statement. Do you really "have to?" What would happen if you didn't? Do you actually have a choice? Notice what happens when you replace "have to" with "get to." When I catch myself, I will literally repeat out loud the same sentence swapping "have to" with "get to." It's surprising how different I feel after saying, "get to" instead. Try it.

From Retail to Coaching

I probably drove SheAh crazy because I kept bouncing back and forth between wanting to focus on Everyday Athlete and deciding my future was in coaching, along with the occasional thought of scrapping both for a secure corporate job. You can probably relate to a time in your life when you were at a crossroads and you went back and forth to the point it made you crazy. It took me six months to reach my final decision.

One of the constants however, was my mindset. It didn't matter if we were discussing Everyday Athlete or my coaching business, I had a negative mindset. I was trapped in thinking Everyday Athlete was doomed. I was worried about having to declare bankruptcy. Worried I would look like a failure. At the same time, I didn't believe in myself as a coach. I worried about not getting clients. I worried about not being good enough for clients if I did get some. A negative mindset is like a runaway train.

Although it took a few months and lots of introspective work on my part, I shifted my thinking. I'll forever be grateful to SheAh for the role he played in helping me turn around my thinking. When I reflect back on the mindset that I was living with for several years I'm speechless. What also stands out to me is how my mindset went from positive to negative very subtly and happened over a period of several years to the point I didn't recognize it and then woke up one day not recognizing myself, and more importantly, not liking myself.

It's analogous to the fact that, on average, Americans gain one pound every year past the age of twenty-five. People go on about their lives, not noticing it, until twenty years later they have bodies they no longer recognize, and wonder where their younger selves went.

I made lists and lists of pros and cons between Everyday Athlete and coaching, consulted trusted friends for advice, ran the numbers, prayed, asked the universe for a sign, flipped a coin, and just about every other thing a person typically does when confronted with a difficult decision. Finally, something happened that made it impossible for me to ignore what I felt in my core but was too afraid to act upon.

Super Soul Sunday

One evening I was watching Oprah's *Super Soul Sunday* and her guest was Jack Canfield, most notably known for the book, *Chicken Soup for the Soul,* which he co-authored with Mark Victor Hansen. They were discussing finding your life's purpose and Jack said, "Your passions are your purpose." As soon as I heard this I shouted internally, "YES!" I paused the program and took out my journal. I knew I was passionate about exercise but as I thought more deeply about it I realized what I've always been most passionate about is helping other people. It is the essence of what fires me up. It's why I've loved fitting people with running shoes for twenty-three years. Friends would always comment, "How can you stand retail?" I've never considered it "retail," but instead considered my work to be helping people find the right running shoes and other gear so they can better enjoy their lives. I love helping other people and making a difference in their lives. Even if it's only the smallest thing but always hoping there is some way I can make a lasting and memorable impact.

After writing several pages of my thoughts, I realized my purpose in life was to empower people to live more fulfilled lives with exercise as the vehicle. Writing helps me connect with my innermost thoughts and feelings. Wanting more information from Jack, I Googled, "Jack Canfield discovering your purpose," where I found more questions to answer. I remember it was a little after 9 p.m. when I began watching that *Super Soul Sunday* episode and it was nearly midnight before I was done writing and discovering my purpose. I completely lost track of time. Before finally turning in to sleep I had refined my purpose, "to inspire people to live more fulfilling lives through exercise and mindset elevation." I read the statement several times over, each time feeling a stronger and stronger connection to my soul and to the universe.

The next morning I woke up feeling the most clear-headed I had felt in a long time. I was also more excited to take on the day than I had been in quite some time. There would be no turning back. My decision was to move forward and build my coaching business.

It's been over a year and a half since I hired my first life coach who helped me change my thinking. I suppose it depends on how you view time. Eighteen months could seem like a long time, yet it goes by very quickly. And perhaps best of all, when you come out on the other side with a completely new outlook on life, it's a very short time. In my case, it was very worth the sacrifices I made. If you were to ask me if it's possible to change our thoughts and if that could lead to changes in our lives, I would say, "Yes!" and my last year and a half is proof.

Elevate Your Mindset, Elevate Your Life

Changing my mindset was one of the more challenging things I've accomplished in my life. SheAh helped me realize that my thinking was negative and he guided me to turn that into thinking positively. When I made my decision to shift my focus away from Everyday Athlete to a coaching career, a friend suggested I meet with a business coach who had helped him recently launch his business.

There is a great Buddhist saying, "When the student is ready, the teacher appears." I took my friend's advice and met with his business coach, Amy Yamada, and decided I could use her help. When I began working with her, she was constantly telling me how I needed to "elevate my mindset." I'll admit it took me awhile to fully agree with her and be willing to commit to the idea. More than a few times I said to her, "What does that even mean - elevate my mindset?" Once I truly understood what she was trying to teach me, things began to change rapidly.

Even though SheAh had helped me turn my overall thinking from predominantly negative to predominantly positive, there was still much work to be done. I was experiencing a feeling I've come to learn is common for many people; that of feeling unworthy. For example, I would often think, "Why would someone want to hire me when they could hire this person or that person?"

It took me several months to allow myself to truly and deeply believe that, yes, I did have value to offer to other people. There was a pivotal moment in my journey when I began to allow myself to think of myself as an expert. I often compared myself to coaches who were much faster and more accomplished than I had ever been, such as Dave Scott who I've considered my triathlon coaching mentor. Dave was instrumental in establishing the sport of triathlon back in its infancy and is a six-time IRONMAN world champion.

One day Amy asked me how many races I had done and our conversation was a slap in the face and light bulb moment wrapped up into one.

Amy: *How many races have you done?*

Me: *Including running races like 5Ks and 10Ks? I don't know. I have no idea.*

Amy: *Just give me a ballpark estimate.*

Me: *I've done nine IRONMAN triathlons. I've done seven marathons. I haven't kept track of my IRONMAN 70.3 races but probably more than twenty-five or thirty. Half Marathons, maybe forty? Maybe fifty? Add in 5Ks and 10Ks, a couple hundred.*

Amy: *Yes. Exactly.*

Me: *But I've been racing for twenty-three years.*

Amy: *Exactly my point. And how many years have you been coaching?*

Me: *Seventeen with Team In Training and twenty overall.*

Amy: *How many athletes have you coached?*

Me: *More than a couple thousand.*

Amy: *You've done hundreds of races to the point you can't count them. You've been coaching for twenty years and* *coached thousands of athletes. Can't you see that to me and the thousands of people like me who've done fewer races than could be counted on one hand, that you are an expert? If you are not an expert, then nobody is.*

After that conversation, it became hard for me to argue I wasn't an expert in triathlon. Most importantly, I experienced a much-needed mental shift and began to see myself as someone who had a lot to offer other people through my coaching. I soon adopted a personal mantra, "Elevate your mindset, elevate your life."

What Makes an Expert Anyway?

I've since come to find out most people I meet feel the same way with respect to their area of expertise. There will always be someone with more knowledge and more impressive results than us in a given field. There's always more to learn; that's part of the joy and what keeps it exciting. That does not mean that we are not an expert or that we don't have valuable lessons to pass on. It does not mean we are not worthy of being a leader or teacher and of being compensated for doing so. I had to work very hard at coming around to the belief that I am worthy of receiving compensation for my knowledge and skill in triathlon coaching.

What makes an expert after all? As Mark Twain said, "An expert is an ordinary fellow from another town." I've come to realize that the person who has the confidence to define themselves as an expert is often unquestioningly and automatically accepted as the expert. A certain amount of confidence is required. It really is all about mindset.

Think about yourself and your skill set for a moment. Are you an expert in something? Odds are that yes, indeed, you are. At the same time, you would probably not classify yourself as an expert. Think about your friends. Are they experts in something? I'd be willing to bet you'd say you have friends who are experts at something, but they would not classify themselves as experts.

When we give ourselves the title of "expert" it places a lot of weight and expectations on our shoulders. Most of us don't want to carry the burden of being an expert and it's easier to deny it. Plus, the minute we say we are an expert at something there surely is someone waiting to challenge us and prove us wrong; or at least that is what we believe. Admitting to yourself for the first time you are an expert brings up all kinds of fears. Fear of failure. Fear of being proved wrong. Fear of needing to step into the role of a leader. Fear of succeeding. Fear of (fill in the blank). The list is endless.

The Merriam-Webster definition of expert is, "having or showing special skill or knowledge because of what you have been taught or what you have experienced."

In this area, I had to work very hard on my internal dialogue to come around to the idea that I am an expert. Amy helped me see and admit to myself that my twenty-three years as a triathlete have taught me a great many lessons I can pass on to others. Completing the USA Triathlon Level I certification course and Dave Scott's Level I and II triathlon coaching certifications for Team In Training have certainly given me a great deal of triathlon knowledge. Reading a dozen or more books on triathlon training methodology has contributed to my knowledge. My nine IRONMAN triathlons and over thirty IRONMAN 70.3 races have given me experience and knowledge. Coaching other athletes for so many years has given me the ability to see what works for different people, to learn from those experiences and to refine my coaching advice. Based on the Merriam-Webster definition how could I not define myself as an expert?

As I have come to understand, I am in expert in the field of triathlon - but none of it matters unless I allow myself to believe I am an expert; that I am a person who has the experience and knowledge to share with others and help them achieve their goals. As mentioned earlier, someone with the confidence to position themselves as an expert becomes an expert. There are plenty of people with less experience, knowledge, and skill but who have a very high degree of self-confidence that do very well for themselves simply because they are not holding themselves back. Many of us, me included, get in our own way. Sometimes the only thing required is to give ourselves permission and get out of our own way.

If there is an area of your life you want to improve or take to a new level, you need to elevate your mindset.

You need to do the work that will allow you to believe you are not only capable of achieving your goals but you are *worthy* of this as well. You need to take control of how you talk to yourself and direct your thoughts instead of letting your thoughts direct you. It's not always easy and it doesn't happen with a snap of your fingers, but it is so worth it when you take control of the space between your ears. Change your thoughts, change your life.

It's an incredible feeling when you are excited about your future and can't wait to begin the next day. Give yourself permission to live a full and exciting life.

LIVE BIG

3

Creating Motivation, Creating Your Life

The power plant doesn't have energy;
it generates energy.

Brendon Burchard

Blowing My Mind

I've been a goal setter my whole life and I've understood that setting goals creates motivation. However, it wasn't until I heard Brendon Burchard's quote that it fully resonated with me. Not only do I have the power to create my own energy and motivation, but I also have the power to create my entire life. To be honest, that was a bit of a mind-blowing concept. "You mean I have the power to create my life? My entire life?"

I've been a person who believed much of life just happened to me and my job was to react and deal with life as best as possible. Now there was someone telling me I could *create* my life. I suppose I should have made this connection much earlier since I created motivation for myself when I took on the challenge of IRONMAN races. To be honest, I never thought of it in that way. Until writing this very paragraph I've always defaulted to the idea that I simply chose an "inspired goal" and it was the goal that created the inspiration and motivation. I failed to make the connection that it was I who created the goal which in turn created the inspiration and the motivation. I suppose I may have failed to make this connection because I felt the book *Unlimited Power* chose me and my decision to do IRONMAN felt like something I was compelled to do as opposed to a logical decision.

I decided to test the idea that I could create anything I wanted in my life. I first thought about all the ways I could create motivation for myself. In fact, I wrote a promotional piece for my triathlon coaching business titled, *My 5 Essentials for Creating Motivation Now!* (I'll provide it with the rest of the Bonus material at the end of the book.) The process of thinking about how I create motivation for myself athletically and how the athletes I coach could put those same principles into place stirred in me all kinds of ideas. I made a short video on the topic too and was surprised when I began to hear from several people about how the idea of creating their own motivation inspired them as well. It seemed to be contagious!

I began to see examples of *creating*, not just motivation, but of creating in every area of life, showing up everywhere; like when you want a new car and suddenly it seems like all you notice on the road is the car you want. I was thinking about Brendon saying energy is generated, and I happened to be watching TV and there was a promo for the Country Music Awards showing Kenny Chesney. I remember thinking, "Damn, he's ripped. What kind of exercise does he do?" Mr. Google led me to an article from *Men's Health* magazine written in 2011 titled, *The Kenny Chesney Workout.* Apparently, he wanted to have more energy so he could put on a better, higher energy concert so he upped his workout regimen. He generated energy by adding high intensity workouts. My first thought, was, "Wouldn't doing a hard workout the day of a concert leave him more tired?" Nope, it created a great deal more energy which he used to give a more energetic performance.

Think about this for a minute. From my experience, most people think exercise only *uses* energy. I hear people talk about how they are too tired to exercise. I hear people say how they would exercise except their jobs are so demanding and they don't have the energy after working all day to exercise.

Maybe exercise also *generates* energy. I thought about all the people I know and asked myself who had more energy, my friends who exercise regularly or my friends who don't exercise. Hands down, no question, my friends who work out have more energy. In fact, those who work out the most seem to have the most energy.

This Brendon character is on to something. Those of us who exercise regularly have more energy. While we use energy, we are also generating and creating more energy. I've been exercising my entire life in one form or another and I had never considered that exercise creates energy. Now that I've been exposed to the concept it seems so obvious. I've had a few friends who have read my initial draft of this book tell me this has been a well-documented fact for decades and "everybody knows this." Well, if that's true then why do so few Americans exercise regularly? If everyone knows that exercise creates energy, wouldn't more people exercise? If everyone understands that exercise increases happiness and feelings of satisfaction, wouldn't more people exercise? I don't believe most people truly understand the connection between exercise and energy creation.

Testing This New Theory

This is a big concept! This idea that we can create anything and everything in our lives; that we are responsible for creating our lives. More than being responsible for the decisions we make and the actions we take, it is taking responsibility to create our reality. It's not just in one area of our lives but in every area. It's some earth-shattering stuff when you start to apply it. Could I be happier? Could I create happiness? Could I create romance? Could I create more fulfilment from my work? I intentionally and successfully created all those things and more in my life simply by focusing on them and deciding to create them!

As I mentioned earlier, I had begun journaling each morning and at the end of each day I decided to rate my day and jot down why I gave it the rating I did. It only took two weeks for me to recognize patterns of when my days were fives to sevens and when my days were eights to tens (on a scale of one to ten).

I noticed when I exercised for at least one hour I consistently had higher rated days. So I realized there was an easy solution - make sure to get an hour of exercise. I also began to identify what was stressing me out and I took measures to reduce my exposure to those situations and people that added stress to my life. I began to plan my tomorrows so they included the experiences and people that created better days, while at the same time reducing and eliminating the negative experiences. I created more happiness by creating more enjoyable days. I created more enjoyable days by planning the night before who and what I wanted my tomorrow to include.

Again, my mind was blown. Lately, most of my not-so-good days are eights. I'm amazed to think the least enjoyable day of my week is an eight while most of my days are nines and tens. Even an eight is a pretty damn great day! With this simple daily practice, I created more happiness in my life.

My practice of rating my day AND identifying WHY led to some of my most profound changes. Plus, it's incredibly easy and takes less than five minutes of your day. All you do is take a few moments toward the end of your day and rate your day using any grading scale that resonates with you (1-5, 1-10, A-F, smiley faces, stars, etc.) I use a 1-10 scale. Then write down why you gave it the rating you did. Within a few days, you will notice patterns of what leads to higher and lower rated days. Next, simply PLAN the things which contribute to your higher rated days and limit or eliminate the things which bring your score down. It's so incredibly powerful. I hope you'll give yourself this gift!

I created more gratefulness in my life by journaling every day about what happened during my day that made me feel grateful. It's the Law of Attraction in action. Simply taking a few minutes at the end of my day to reflect on a few key moments or experiences allows me to revisit them and reminds me of the blessings in my life. When I put myself in this state of gratefulness I instantly feel a calming presence and I am reminded of how fortunate I am. I am in excellent health and I get to use my body every day to do what I love - exercise. I have a wonderful marriage to the love of my life and when I reflect on our relationship it reminds me how lucky I am to share my life with Janine. I do my best to remind myself every day how much joy and happiness she adds to my life.

Relationships can be self-fulfilling prophecies in that how we view a relationship affects how we treat the relationship and the person, which in turn changes how we feel about and view the relationship. The pattern repeats itself over and over. Take a moment and think about one of your most important relationships. Now think about all the things about this person which annoy you, frustrate you, drive you crazy, and maybe even make you angry. If you are focusing on these attributes when you first see this person at the end of a long day, how are you going to greet them? Now think about all the aspects of this person you admire, respect, love, and cherish. When you're in this frame of mind, how do you think you will treat this person when you first see them after a long day? Your reaction to this person will absolutely be different based on the focus you are holding in your mind. These interactions shape the relationship. This is precisely why my focus on gratefulness for all the wonderful ways Janine adds enjoyment to my life helps me better interact with her, which in turn gives us a stronger relationship.

I've learned that if I want our marriage to have more romance I can create it. On several occasions, I've decided to make my wife a delicious dinner and have it waiting for her upon her return from work, complete with a candlelight table setting. Sometimes I get her a card for no reason other than to show her I love her. Every time I do something special for Janine, I end up getting as much and typically more in return.

This is a key lesson I hope you take from this chapter, so let me repeat it. If you want something in your life and relationships, create it. So often in relationships we want the other person to make the sacrifice, we want the other person to do the work or take the first step. When we think this way, we have it all backwards. It's up to us to create that which we desire. We will get what we want out of the relationship when we deliver it to the other person first. If you want better friendships, become a better friend!

Testing the Theory on Others

The athletes I coach will tell you I am always relating concepts of triathlon to life. What can I say, it's my thing. Life is about so much more than triathlon. Every time I find something that brings my life to a higher level of enjoyment I share those strategies and exercises with the athletes I coach as well as my friends. When they experience the same amazing results that I do and they share their success stories with me, those moments are priceless.

While I was writing this book, Janine and I went to Washington, D.C. to visit our dear friends Kathryn and

Nathan and their two-year-old son, Tyler. One day while Janine and Kathryn were outside playing with Tyler, Nathan asked me, "What's new? What's up with you?" I excitedly told him about this book which included all of the concepts and exercises that I've implemented into my life that have allowed me to experience so much growth in my life. Nathan was genuinely interested so I offered to send him the rough draft of my book.

A few weeks later Nathan and I talked on the phone and he was telling me about the changes in his life which came from reading my book as well as implementing a few of the techniques. I was over the moon with excitement. "Wow! These words I've written are having an effect and bringing positive outcomes to my friend Nathan. I can't wait to share it with the rest of the world!" It was so encouraging. I asked Nathan to tell you in his own words what he experienced.

Lance and I happened to discuss the idea of creating energy when I was looking for a way to do that. It seemed more difficult each day to balance all the areas of my life. The important parts in my day-to-day life were not letting up. My evenings were jam-packed with family time and work. I would think tomorrow would be different and I would have time to start working out again. I'd been fighting this for a few years. I had been taken out of my normal exercise routine by a ski accident and back surgery leaving me with chronic back pain. My normal runs of six to eight miles became walks around the block. After talking with Lance I realized there was a better way.

I started setting my alarm clock to give me an hour of extra time in the morning. I started with an hour of yoga, strengthening workouts, and daily push-ups for a couple weeks, and then my first run. It was a very short run, but it was a run. The best part was that I was able to do it again the next day, and the day after that. Soon I was doing more running than I had done in years. I found myself moving my alarm earlier to create more time for my workouts while finding myself with more energy for my family in the evenings.

I really noticed the difference the first time we had guests in town. It was a busy week of kids, zoos, and museums. The extra people in the house left little room for my morning routine, and it was bumped from the daily schedule. By the time the guests left, I was dragging, sluggish, and my lower back pain had returned. It took a week or so of my morning time routine to get back to the energy I had recently found.

Big Magic

I've read that eighty to ninety percent of Americans dream of writing a book. I have no idea if that is accurate; I haven't found any scientific studies backing up this statistic, but it is often repeated. Maybe it's accurate, maybe it's completely fabricated, I can't tell you. But I can tell you it was true for me. The idea of a book written by me . . . I thought it was cool as hell. But I also thought there was as much of a chance of writing a book as winning the

Kentucky Derby. I've never seriously considered the idea, that is, up until less than two years ago.

I've been absolutely experiencing what Elizabeth Gilbert calls "Big Magic." Big things, sometimes unexplainable coincidences were happing in my life (and still are!) and at exceedingly increasing speeds too. The universe has clearly been sending me a message. Actually, it has been sending me all kind of messages. I just need to keep working on receiving the messages.

As she points out in her book, *Big Magic,* it's our job to hear these messages and invite them into our lives and yes, as scary as it is, take action on them. Perhaps one of my first Big Magic moments happened before I had even heard of the concept or even listened to her podcast appropriately called *Magic Lessons*.

I first met Allison back in 2001 when she was an athlete on the first triathlon team I coached for Team In Training. She had not lived in Seattle for quite some time and was just in town for a week or so on a consulting gig for her former employer. It was one of those rare but treasured late September days in Seattle with not a cloud in the sky. Her vacation rental overlooked Lake Washington and the deck had an amazing view of Mt. Rainier. She invited Janine and me over for an evening barbecue and it turned out to be a night that completely altered my future. In fact, if not for that night I honestly believe I would not have written this book.

She asked how my triathlon coaching was coming along and I shared with her it was a struggle. Allison told me she thought I would really love this book called *The Millionaire Messenger* by Brendon Burchard. In fact, she made me promise her I would read it. She also gave the names of two other books to read, *The Miracle Morning* by Hal Elrod and *The Big Leap* by Gay Hendricks. Since Allison is one of the most brilliant people I know, there was no question whether I would read these books; it was only a matter of when. I read two of them straight away. All three books had an immediate and enormous impact on the transformation I've undergone over the last couple of years.

The Millionaire Messenger is the book that first started me thinking about telling my story by writing a book. I really connected with the idea of "the power of story" and how every person's story has the power to positively affect another person, and even change their life. This same theme began to show up for me as I listened to the podcasts of Hal Elrod and Liz Gilbert. I was deeply inspired listening to Hal talk about how writing his book allowed him to share his story and connect on a deeper level with so many more people. Knowing that I want to impact as many people as possible, writing a book became a logical next step. The *Magic Lessons* podcast was influential because I heard Liz interview people and learn how when we begin a creative project and release it into the universe, magical, seemingly unexplained coincidences appear. The path forward unfolds and we learn we don't need to know in advance every little step regarding how something is going to happen. It seemed everywhere I turned the universe was telling me to share my story because the telling of it would benefit others.

I began to consider that just maybe my story had value to other people. I began writing my story and forming the early portions of a possible book. I found as I began to share parts of my story with friends, they were telling me they found it inspiring. The shift in my mind had begun. "Maybe I could write a book that would be worth reading and would add value to other people's lives." As I allowed myself to be vulnerable with people and open up about my dreams and aspirations for writing a book as well as my hopes and plans for my coaching business I noticed some interesting things happening in my life.

All of a sudden I learned that one of my athletes, Stacie, was an editor in the technical writing field and she agreed to look at my book and makes suggestions. Facebook friends suggested various leads on how to go about writing and publishing a book. The more I shared with people about what I was working on, the more seemingly unexplainable events occurred which kept moving my book project forward. Then the completely unexpected happened.

The Book Unexpected

After completing the introduction and a few chapters and getting feedback from Stacie, I began to investigate what it would take to get it published. I sent it off to several publishers including one that specializes in endurance sports. It got rejected. No surprise, what author doesn't have a rejection story or two? My wife's cousin, Bill Carter, who's had several books published (check out my personal favorite *Boom, Bust, Boom: A Story About Copper, The Metal That Runs The World*) half-jokingly told me, "Only forty more rejections to go." Bill has been an inspiration to me since I've known him because he's passionately pursued his book and film projects relentlessly. I've learned from him when it comes to getting creative projects published and produced it is not an easy road but ultimately worth the hardships along the way.

At some point in the process while tracking down every lead suggested by my friends and social media, I met with Patty Pacelli of Pacelli Publishing which conveniently is located just across Lake Washington in Bellevue, Washington. As I was telling Patty about *Live Big* she told me about her company's Six-Word Lessons Series where each book in the series is a collection 100 lessons on a specific topic. A light bulb went off. Surely, I can write 100 lessons on triathlon I thought to myself. That night I went home and began brainstorming and before I knew it I had eighty-three ideas and it was nearly 1 a.m.! I found myself completely absorbed, creative juices flowing and utterly unaware of time. A little more than three months later *Six-Word Lessons for Successful Triathletes: 100 Lessons for Essential Training and Racing* was finished and published.

How crazy is that? Before I even finished what I consider to be my first book (the one you are reading), I found myself a published author. That my friends is Big Magic!

The reason for sharing that story is to encourage you to listen to your inner voice and to share your hopes, dreams, and aspirations with others. You never know who or what the universe has in store for you, but you'll never find out if you don't summon the courage to begin.

When it comes to creating our lives, it really does come down to what we do consistently. As Aristotle so intelligently said, "We are what we repeatedly do. Excellence, then, is not an act, but a habit."

4

Using Habits to Design Our Lives

Being miserable is a habit; being happy is a habit; and the choice is yours.

Tom Hopkins

Identifying Habits

Take a moment to evaluate your life. Are you excited with your life? How happy are you? What kind of physical shape are you in? What is your financial state? How's your love life? How are your friendships? Are there areas you would like to improve or strengthen? Is there something missing from your life that you desire? Go ahead . . . put down the book, break out some paper and pen and write. I'll be here waiting for you when you are finished.

Take any one area that you want to focus on and write down your habits in this area. What do you do daily that is related to this area of your life? What are the thoughts you repeatedly think regarding this area of your life? What are your beliefs about yourself or what you may or may not be worthy of related to this area of your life? Return to your pen and paper and write down everything that comes to mind. Get it all out and down on paper so you can review it.

Awareness is often the first step toward change. The tricky thing about habits is that they've become so ingrained and automatic we are barely aware of them. We've taken the same actions, thought the same thoughts, and held the same beliefs over and over to the point that we do them unconsciously. Our realities are the result of our habits, which are the result of our actions, which are the result of our thoughts, which are the result of our beliefs. If our beliefs, thoughts, actions, and habits are delivering us results that we do not want, then we need to disrupt the chain of events and create new patterns.

Expand your awareness beyond what you do, think, and believe to the actions you don't take but need to; the thoughts you don't think but need to; the beliefs you don't currently have but know you need to develop. By identifying the habits you need to put in place, you will have the framework needed to get the results you desire. This same exercise will also help you create your own personal affirmations which will remind you of the new course you are charting for your life.

Creating Affirmations

This exercise is most effective when you concentrate on one area of your life that you want to improve. When you have identified the area you want to concentrate on, identified your habits, actions, thoughts, and beliefs, and written them down so you can review them, you're ready to get started.

The first step is to review everything you've written down. Now separate everything into two categories; the positive beliefs, thoughts, actions, and habits that contribute to the results you want and the negative aspects that are limiting you.

Review your positive column and ask yourself if you can strengthen what you've written. Is there a belief or thought you can make stronger and more powerful? Is there an action that could increase or improve the results you want? Is there a beneficial habit you already possess that could be strengthen or done more frequently? Sometimes to get the desired results, we simply need to strengthen the positive and increase the frequency of the beliefs, thoughts, actions, and habits that support us. Take a moment and rewrite any of these statements you've decided you can strengthen. If it's a matter of increasing the frequency for any of your statements, write down your plan for how and when you will add these to your life. Schedule them into your life; add them to your calendar and set up reminders.

Next, review your negative column. Review those beliefs, thoughts, actions, and habits that prevent you from attaining the results you desire. Rewrite ALL of them so they serve you and add value to your life. Examine them, challenge them, and reframe them. Write them in a way that will serve you moving forward and not limit you. If rewriting them in a positive way causes you to feel inauthentic, use Bridge Statements and go at your own pace, but keep moving forward toward the positive.

All the statements that you have rewritten and strengthened are now your personal affirmations and you can repeat them to yourself to create new habits that will lead you to the results you want. Write them on post-it notes and place them where you'll see them every day such as your bathroom mirror, nightstand, or at work.

Often, the affirmation you need most can be found in your greatest pain.

My Greatest Hang-up

Growing up I learned pretty early on that my father was interested in spending time with me as long as the activity was something *he* was interested in. The problem was that he and I were interested in different things. He loved working on race cars and I loved ball sports. When I was a young boy, somewhere around eight years old, I remember getting a new baseball glove for Easter and all I wanted to do was play catch with my dad. I remember bugging him every night when he got home from work to play catch with me. "Maybe this weekend." "Not tonight, I have to work on the race car." On and on it went.

Finally, I gave up asking. One day I found that if I threw the baseball up on to the roof of the house, as it rolled down it would hit the eave over the front porch and come flying off in a different direction every time which forced me to react as the ball would disappear from my view and pop up into the air. "What great practice!" I thought to myself. I was quite pleased with this game I had created for myself.

My dad came home from work one day while I was playing catch with myself and completely ripped me a new one, going off about how I was destroying the roof. I interpreted that sequence of events (along with the many other instances of my dad not being interested in my passions) to mean that he was not interested in me. I further interpreted that to mean that I was not worthy of his interest, and therefore his love.

My father's main "language" was money; every-thing was about money. I damaged myself psychologically by deciding that if I was not worthy of his interest and his love then I was also not worthy of money. I realize that logically this makes no sense, but on an emotional level it was etched into the core of who I believed I was.

When I realized that I did not feel worthy of money I went deep inside to see what other areas I might feel unworthy. To my surprise this was the only area that jumped out at me. I've always felt worthy of friendship and had tremendous friendships growing up that I still have today. I've always felt worthy of love as my mom more than made up for the love I did not receive from my dad. I've always felt worthy of succeeding at sports, education, jobs, etc. because I've always equated success with putting in the necessary work. Feeling unworthy of money is the thing I am most haunted by. It's the dragon I most need to slay. It's my great white whale.

When I did the exercise for creating affirmations, I began with: "I am not worthy of interest and wealth." I changed that statement and created several new ones for myself.

- "I am worthy of interest because I am interested in others."

- "I am worthy of wealth because I add massive value to people's lives."

- "I am extremely supportive and encouraging of others."

- "I constantly strive to inspire and motivate others and help them live more fulfilled lives."

- "I am worthy of wealth because I enrich other people's lives."

My limiting belief that I was not worthy of my father's interest and therefore wealth created my daily thoughts of unworthiness and ultimately created limiting beliefs, actions, and habits which have prevented me from attracting wealth. I've been coaching athletes for over twenty years and for the vast majority of that time I've charged either very little or nothing for my coaching. It's only been in the last year that I've begun charging for my coaching in earnest. To be honest, I still have people telling me I am not charging enough and that my knowledge, skills and services are worth more. *Baby steps, but still forward progress.*

With my new affirmations, I've been able to shift my mindset. I've begun to create new actions which will lead to new habits which will lead to a new reality for me in the area of wealth. It's not always comfortable for me to take these new actions of charging people money for my coaching, but I realize they are necessary for me to live into my best self.

We all have our demons and challenges. I'm no different than you. Except for maybe the fact I just spilled one of my darkest, deepest insecurities. I must say, it feels incredibly vulnerable and raw, but also liberating. I can only hope that exposing my insecurity will encourage you to examine your own limiting beliefs and inspire you to challenge them so you can move beyond them. I have to believe a better life is waiting for all of us once we cross through the pain.

How to be Unhappy

Negative things are going to happen to us; it's part of life. The difference depends on whether we allow ourselves to perpetually live in a negative state or if we consciously choose to be the director of our lives. Let's take a moment and use negativity to illustrate how we can choose how we live. Write down everything that you can think of that would cause you to live a chronically unhappy life. Here's the list I wrote for myself. Feel free to use this, and add your own.

1. Think negatively.

2. Assume the worst in others. View the world and all people as out to get me.

3. Be rude. Don't smile, say "thank you," or be kind to others.

4. Do not exercise.

5. Eat a diet primarily comprised of processed carbohydrates and little to no fruits and vegetables.

6. Drink soda instead of water.

7. Focus on all the things in life that are lacking.

8. Worry constantly.

9. Blame others for my unhappiness, lack of success, and basically everything.

10. Complain constantly - about everything and everyone.

11. Do not learn new things and never consider another point of view.

12. Expect anyone I have a relationship to take the first step, to make the invitation, to call me, and to plan any get-together.

13. Dwell on all my flaws and shortcomings. View everything that does not work out as expected as failure which reinforces that I am a failure.

The list taken in its entirety may seem over the top and extreme, but how many of us practice at least one or two of these habits on a consistent basis? It's very easy to see that any person who made a daily habit of practicing all of these would indeed be very miserable. Simply living each day with only a couple of these attributes will drag a person down. Why not choose to live the opposite of the list above?

Why is it difficult for humans to believe that if they made a daily habit of practicing the opposite of these negative habits, they could live a joyous life? Is it that practicing the positive version appears to take "too much effort?" Sometimes it just takes a realization that we are choosing to actively engage in destructive behavior.

Go through my list, or better yet, create your own list of habits you would need to live the worst version of yourself. Now write down the opposite; take every statement and create its opposite. Create a list of principles by which you are committed to living your life. Carry them with you on note cards or your phone so you can revisit them each day. Remind yourself of the life you aspire to live. Do your best each day to live that life and before you know it, you will be living as your best self.

Habits of Training and Racing Outcomes

With each new Team In Training season I coach, there are athletes who, after months of training, come to the race with more than eighty percent of the training schedule completed. Unfortunately, there are also a few who show up at the race with barely twenty percent completed. Things came up, life got in the way, and they just couldn't train on a consistent basis. I'm guessing it will not surprise you to know that the group that did more than eighty percent of the training schedule had better race performances.

Now, it doesn't mean the athletes who did not train consistently are bad people or that I am judging them; it simply means training was not a priority in their life. Consequently, their race became a reflection of their training. In fact, the same can be said for most people's race experiences, whether good or bad.

I will fully confess I was guilty of this on many occasions. For many years, I was disappointed in my race results. I would have a goal in mind for a race, and I would come up short of that goal and beat myself up for it. It wasn't until after one particular race when I sat down and honestly evaluated my training that I realized I did, in fact, have the race I had trained for. My results were an honest outcome of my training. I simply did not do the training required to achieve the result I wanted. I realized my disappointment was misplaced. Instead of being disappointed in my performance I realized my disappointment needed to be placed at the feet of my training. Understanding the disappointment belonged to my training meant that I could improve my training for the next race and allow my results to speak for the training. This experience led me to create one of my favorite sayings to share with the athletes I coach, "Focus on the effort and the results will take care of themselves."

Frustration and disappointment set in when our expectations and our outcomes don't align. Sometimes they don't align because of our performance. However, if we are honest with ourselves, we'll most often see the primary reason has far more to do with our preparation.

Take a moment and think about an area of your life where you are frustrated or disappointed in your results, your outcomes, or your current situation. You are probably frustrated because you want things to be different. Honestly assess if you've done the necessary preparation to achieve a higher set of outcomes. Have you done all that is required? Have you been consistent in making a daily practice out of these things? Have you held yourself to a high enough standard? Have you given yourself enough time to achieve the results you want? Do your results accurately reflect your preparation? If the answer is, "Yes, I could have done more," then you can let go of frustration and disappointment and focus on the areas you can improve.

At the very least you can shift your disappointment from your performance and outcomes to frustration about your preparation. This is a critical shift because you can then change, adapt, and improve your preparation which will lead to improved results. If you solely focus on your disappointing outcomes, then you'll prepare in the same fashion and you'll likely experience falling short in your desired results which will lead to more disappointment. On and on the cycle repeats itself.

Ever since I had the epiphany of evaluating my training honestly when reviewing my race results, I've never been disappointed in my performance. I have occasionally been disappointed in my training that led up to the race; however, this provided motivation to train more thoroughly moving forward. My race results have been in direct alignment with my training.

The Power of a Training Log

Make it a daily habit to keep a training log. The simple act of recording your training will help you hold yourself accountable, which will in turn increase the likelihood of achieving your goals. There are many ways beyond a training log to implement systems of accountability into your training, such as training partners, group workouts, classes, coaches, social media, and races.

Your training log holds you accountable because when you skip a workout or shorten it and then have to record that into your log, it forces acknowledgment. Using a training log each day keeps you focused on your goals and your progress. You either have done the work you planned or you haven't, and your training log makes you keenly aware of your progress and journey. Admitting we are behind or not doing the work we agreed to helps create focus moving forward. The training log also provides positive feedback. When we log our well-performed workouts, we feel better and more optimistic about our training moving forward, as well as our upcoming races. This in turn generates excitement and motivation.

Motivation is another key benefit of keeping a training log. Often just the idea of knowing that you are going to be logging an entry, or for that matter logging a zero, is enough to get you out of the door and into your workout. Starting can be half the battle. Countless workouts have been completed simply because the athlete did not want to admit not doing the workout in the training log.

Developing the habit of keeping a training log will deliver accountability, motivation, and other benefits. Training logs provide better and more objective reviews of your training than memory alone. They are excellent tools for measuring progress. It's easy to compare the data of a workout that you've done multiple times. Your training log allows you to go back and accurately extract this data. As you record key metrics, like speed or pace, it's easy to review your log and discover how you are performing compared to past performances.

Nothing helps predict a race performance like review of critical workouts and overall training trends. Training logs can also help you plan future training sessions. If what you did last season resulted in your best season, repeat what you did. If last season did not go as planned what lessons can you learn by reviewing your past training? What can you change or improve? Your training log holds the answers.

All these benefits are yours when you make a habit of recording your training on a daily basis. A training log is a microcosm of life. Small, daily, and seemingly inconsequential actions lead to much bigger results.

Wise Words from Mike

You've probably heard the phrase, "Showing up is half the battle." Every single person I know has days when they simply don't want to exercise. So often, the hardest part is simply getting started. The same is true for most things in life, not only exercise. Here's my friend Mike telling a little bit of his story.

Having taken up triathlon later in life at the age of 35, and never really being a swimmer or cyclist, I didn't know what IRONMAN was really about. Thanks to the guidance of Lance and some great training partners (including my wife) I eventually competed in four full distance triathlons. I am very proud to say I even broke the twelve-hour mark. If I have taken anything from my time in the sport it is this: First and foremost is getting to the starting line. I use this mantra all the time in my daily life. If all you do is look at the myriad of things you have to do in any given day, oftentimes it gets overwhelming. Sometimes it's so overwhelming you fail to even start, or you distract yourself with other tasks that you convince yourself are important but are really nothing more than distractions and procrastination.

Secondly, it is not the finish that matters but the process of getting there. Commit to the training and the race will take care of itself. Consistency pays off.

Whether it's a race, or work, or family, just get started. To put it in terms of completing a full distance triathlon, don't think about the last thirteen miles of the marathon while you are swimming. I often start each day with a quick little reminder to myself, "Get to the starting line." Then I jump out of bed and go about my day.

The idea of just getting started has gotten me out the door for many workouts. This idea was tip number 63 in my book *Six-Word Lessons for Successful Triathletes: 100 Lessons for Essential Training and Racing:*

Lesson 63: If motivation to run is low . . . just run for 15 minutes. If after 15 minutes you still don't feel like running then call it a day. Typically you will begin to feel better within 10 minutes and you'll decide that you want to keep going. Starting is often the hardest part. Make a deal with yourself to begin before deciding to cancel a run.

One of the triathletes I coach named Josh Cooper owns a fitness boot camp gym in Kirkland called *Embody Health.* He told me that since he read that lesson in my book he's been sharing it with his clients, with great success. One of the main reasons his clients do group high intensity training is because they know they won't work out on their own. However, even with a group they still struggle occasionally. Josh gets his clients to commit to just doing the first ten minutes and then allows them to stop if they still don't feel like exercising. Fortunately, that rarely happens.

The Power of Questions

I first learned about a guy named Jon Bergoff while listening to Hal Elrod's podcast, episode 107 titled, *A Radical Approach to Achieving Your 2016 Goals.* This episode is also the first time I had ever heard of the event, "The Best Year Ever (Blueprint)" which I would, unknowingly at the time, attend eleven months later.

Jon's approach to living life through asking yourself empowering questions is brilliant and it's been an extremely successful tactic for me in creating better results for myself as well as the athletes I coach. Let me share how I have increased productivity by following lessons I've learned from Jon.

First, let's begin with something simple yet profound. When we tell ourselves we cannot do something, the brain accepts this as truth and does not devote any time to finding a solution. On the other hand, when we ask ourselves an open-ended question, a question we don't even need to answer, the brain sets about searching for answers. Often, our minds will deliver an answer while we sleep. Have you ever had a "brilliant" idea or previously unconsidered solution come to you in the middle of the night while you were sound asleep? It's happened to me on so many occasions that I'll often go to sleep, asking myself an open-ended question right before bed, just to let my subconscious go to work.

Here is an example I see constantly. One person will say, "I want to do a triathlon," and one of their friends will say, "I could never do a triathlon because I don't know how to swim." To that friend, it's a foregone conclusion and they will never attempt a triathlon. What if that friend instead said, "I can't do a triathlon right now because I can't swim. But what if I could learn how to swim?" Now, the possibility of doing a triathlon is on the table because the only barrier is learning how to swim. The brain will begin to notice cues that it otherwise would have ignored such as a comment from a colleague about learning how to swim. This prompts a question and a dialogue about learning to swim which leads to the contact information of a swim coach who specializes in teaching adults to swim. Or the friend wonders what it would take to learn to swim and has the idea to ask the local community pool if they offer adult swim classes. If you want to do something but don't know how, just ask yourself an open-ended question and let your subconscious go to work. For example, "What would it look it if I could _____?"

My most productive journaling sessions come when I begin by asking myself a question. Prior to being introduced to Jon I would break out my notebook and simply start writing down my thoughts. Now, I begin by writing down a question for myself. I've also learned that I can improve my journaling sessions even more if, before diving straight into journaling, I examine the question I've written down and see if I can improve the question. I hear Jon's voice reminding me to, "Ask a better, more thorough question." Let me give you an example.

"How can I become a better coach?" Instead, what if I asked myself, "How can I best serve the athletes I coach?" The first question is more focused on me and the second question is focused more on the athletes. I could improve the question further by changing it to, "How can I best serve the athletes I coach by discovering their needs?" I could even deepen the question, "How can I best serve the athletes I coach by discovering their needs AND find ways to lead, educate. encourage, motivate, challenge and inspire them?"

I have a set of questions I've printed in the first pages of my daily journal. I read them before beginning my journaling because reading them and answering them puts me in an incredibly empowering state of mind. Here they are:

- What could my life look like, such that I would live fully alive?

- What are three things I am completely excited about manifesting in my future?

- Who do I need to become in order to live into this vision of myself and my life?

- What one characteristic embodies who I need to become and how I need to show up?

Answer the questions above for yourself, and better yet, create your own questions that will empower you to live your best life.

Design Your Life

We often say we want one thing while our consistent actions prove otherwise. We all face this battle at some point and in some aspect of our lives. As my friend Amy likes to remind me, "You can tell a person's priorities by how they spend their money and their time." Think about that for a moment. Where, how and with whom do you spend your time? How do you spend your money? If you want to experience a different type of life, then make different choices about how you spend your money and time.

The beauty of the situation is that you have the power to choose. You have the power to create the life you want. We often make it seem so difficult when all we have to do is set up our life one day at a time. Consciously choose how you are going to spend your time. Then repeat those choices every day until you form habits. We all have habits - some good, and some bad. Half the time we don't even realize what our habits actually are. Take some time right now to think about the direction you want your life to go.

What do you want? In fact, take out a sheet of paper or your journal and write down what kind of life you want to live.

- How do you want to earn your living such that you will create maximum value for yourself and others?

- What type of relationships do you want to create in order to design your best life?

- How do you want to spend your time such that you will live without regret?

- What passions do you want to pursue so that you can live big?

- What type of people do you want to surround yourself with; people who would help you become the best version of yourself?

- What's missing in your life that would elevate your life to a new, higher level?

Now, focus on just one area of your life. After you have identified what you want for that area and you have clarity about what you desire, ask yourself another set of questions. There are no wrong answers; they are simply guideposts to plan your roadmap as you move forward.

- What are your habits regarding this area?

- What are you doing consistently in your thoughts and actions regarding this area of your life?

- What are you NOT doing but need to do to achieve what you desire?

- What's holding you back from achieving what you desire?

- How do you spend your time and your money regarding this area of your life?

Answering these questions truthfully will reveal what changes you need to make, and more importantly, what habits you need to create. Create the habit and the habit will create the result.

Now, set about designing your life by designing your day. Plan your thoughts. Premeditate your actions. Set up "triggers" to remind yourself throughout your day. I learned the following excellent trigger from one of Brendon's courses: Take out your smartphone and create an alarm that goes off every day. Label the alarm with a question or statement that will help keep you on track.

I have several that go off each day. One of them is a reminder to me on how I want to show up in the world and it reads, "Magnify Enthusiasm and Inspiration." I did an exercise once where I listed all the qualities I wanted to exhibit as a person. I found I was living all of the qualities I wrote down, but I also realized I was not living them to the extent I wanted to. That's when I decided to "turn up the volume." I imagined the volume dial on a stereo and I saw myself cranking it up. "Magnify Enthusiasm and Inspiration" succinctly captured my desire to live my life at a higher level. I remind myself daily of this experience and this desire to turn up the volume on my life. "Magnify Enthusiasm and Inspiration" pops up on my phone daily and it's most often the phrase I write in my journal when I ask myself how I want to show up in the world today.

What smartphone trigger can you set for yourself right now? What one quality, characteristic, or idea do you want to remind yourself of daily?

When we do things without consciously deciding, that's habit in action. The best news is that we have the power to create habits that empower our goals. We just need to decide, and then take consistent action each day until the act no longer requires conscious thought; until it becomes *habit*.

My Daily Journal

Perhaps the thing that has changed my life more than anything this past year has been the creation of my daily journal. More specifically, it's been the daily habit of utilizing the journal. I've written a bonus chapter titled "30 Day Challenge" at the end of this book that is designed to help you create your own daily journal and success formula. I would also recommend that you read *The Miracle Morning* and create your own morning success ritual.

In my reading, I noticed that several of the leaders in personal development had morning routines. I decided to create my own morning routine which evolved over the first few weeks as I went through several iterations. I am a person who gets more accomplished when I write things down and create checklists for myself rather than log them into a computer or use a phone app so I created my own daily journal. I used Adobe Illustrator to create a document that would guide me each morning in my routine. At first I would print just a few copies and use them up. I would keep all the elements that worked for me and change up those that were not serving me. Once I had developed a routine that I enjoyed I printed off fifty sheets of my journal, front and back, and took it to a print shop to have them cut and bind the sheets, creating my own personal journal. Each morning I simply needed to open my journal to a fresh day, check off the activities and use the journal to write down my thoughts. Here's a run-down of my morning routine.

Upon waking up I do three modified sun salutations as this limbers up my body and makes me feel so much better. I then do one of my ten-minute physical therapy strength training routines. Next, I do five minutes of meditation and five minutes of visualization while listening to the sound of waves crashing on a beach. I imagine I am sitting on beach in Hawaii - calm, peaceful, rested, and relaxed. Life is good!

After my meditation/visualization I spend about fifteen minutes writing in my journal where I list the major projects I am working on, the day's priority list, and what I am going to do for exercise. I once read that when people list the specific type of exercise they plan to do and the time they plan to do it, they're more successful at completing it. So, I write down what I am going to do for exercise and when.

I write down the person I want to be and the energy I want to bring to my day. I write down reminders such as, "Magnify Enthusiasm and Inspiration" or "Live Big." Then I write down my affirmations and do my "positive journaling."

It's funny to me now, how much I struggled with writing anything positive about myself and now I fill several lines in a couple of minutes with so much positivity that if you didn't know my story and only read my positive journaling you'd think I was completely in love with myself.

That's my morning routine which takes about forty minutes. I'm not perfect - I sometimes miss a day and there have been times I've missed a couple of weeks. What I find most interesting is that the more days I miss, the more I begin to feel like I used to feel; more negative, more stressed out, and less excited about life. The routine of my daily journal has become similar to exercise in the sense that if I miss it for the day I am noticeably less fulfilled.

At night I spend another ten to fifteen minutes of specific journaling, because a great tomorrow really begins the night before. Before going to bed I journal on the following questions:

- What happened today that I am grateful for?

- Celebrate my accomplishments. What can I celebrate today?

- How would I rate today and why?

- What am I excited about/looking forward to tomorrow?

Doing any part of this daily routine will elevate your life; doing all of these elements on a daily basis will dramatically improve the quality of your life. Think about it - exercise, meditation, visualization, journaling, appreciation, gratefulness, reminding yourself of your accomplishments, and looking forward to the next day - every one of those things individually leads to a more enjoyable life. Doing all of them every day is life-changing.

One of the coolest things that happened to me when I began journaling came from answering the question, "How would I rate today and why?" Within two weeks it became readily apparent that certain activities during the day gave that day a lower score. And there were certain things that led to higher scores when they were included in my day. It doesn't take a rocket scientist to realize that if I wanted to live a happier, more fulfilled life, I should plan for and include the things that drove the rating up and reduce or eliminate those things that drove the score down. Almost immediately upon that recognition, along with the changes in my daily activities, my scores zoomed higher.

It's hard to argue with a system and routine that can have you living at a nine or ten on a scale of one to ten nearly every day of your life! I have so much to enjoy and appreciate in my life and it's an incredible feeling. I truly hope you feel the same way. If you don't, I hope you will challenge yourself to elevate your habits and routines and take your life to an entirely new level.

5

Community: The People We Surround Ourselves With

What should young people do with their lives today? Many things, obviously. But the most daring thing is to create stable communities in which the terrible disease of loneliness can be cured.

Kurt Vonnegut

It's Really About Connecting

Take a moment and think about what you really want in your life. Review the list you made for yourself from the last chapter under, "Design Your Life." As you made your list and described your life, did you picture yourself isolated and alone without anyone to share it with? Or does the vision of your best life include sharing it with a loved one, family and friends? What are some of your most wonderful memories? I'd be willing to bet they include other people and not just you.

Deep down we want to create connections and shared experiences with other people. These shared connections and experiences enrich our lives. The deeper the connections, the more meaningful the relationships.

Endurance sports such as running and triathlon create these connections naturally. There is the saying, "Misery loves company." Suffering through tough workouts and races create strong bonds among athletes. Humans naturally bond with others when sharing sacrifice and suffering. Of course, sacred bonds are also created through shared joy and happiness.

When you meet up with an old friend you haven't seen in a while, how often does the following phrase come up, "Remember that time when . . .?" You're recalling a shared experience which brings up the feeling of connection. That's the beauty of training and racing with friends - you experience both the lows and the highs together; each making the friendship stronger.

"Sometimes you will never know the value of a moment until it becomes a memory." – Dr. Seuss

Maybe it was Destiny

Looking back on that fateful day of July 31, 1993, I can't believe it's been over twenty-three years. I am also amazed at how that one day set my life upon a path I never expected, and at the same time am incredibly grateful for. Had I not done my first triathlon, perhaps I never would have had the desire to live a life that included exercise as a major component. Maybe I never would have asked myself, "What else can I accomplish?" I certainly don't think I would have looked for work in a running store and I'm sure I would not have become a triathlon coach. Coaching athletes allows me to make a difference in other people's lives. Oftentimes it appears to me the difference I make is quite small and then unexpectedly I get an email from someone telling me I changed their life. When I hear news like this I am as astounded as I am excited - part disbelief and part over the moon with pride and joy. I feel incredibly fortunate to be able to connect with people through the sport of triathlon. As I mentioned previously, triathlon is just my vehicle - my vehicle to live a greater purpose and to make a difference in other people's lives.

Had I not gone to work at the running store in Seattle, I'm certain the Washington/Alaska Chapter of The Leukemia and Lymphoma Society never would have contacted me to implement their very first triathlon program back in the year 2000. Connecting with so many people throughout my time as a Team In Training (TNT) coach has been life-changing for me. Aside from the close friends I grew up with, the vast majority of my friends have come into my life through TNT. There is something about the process and experience of training alongside people for several months and then sharing a destination race weekend that creates strong bonds. It's not just my own experience either. This is a common sentiment throughout the TNT community.

Madison

It's also not totally unique to Team In Training. I have several friends who belong to various local triathlon clubs and it's clear they too share this special bond among their teammates.

In September of 2016 I was honored when a group of eighteen triathletes who trained together as part of Stoke Multisport all chipped in to pay for my travel expenses so I could join them in Madison for IRONMAN Wisconsin. While I was only coaching five of the triathletes, I had supported the whole team on their last long bike ride (112 miles) three weeks earlier. I drove up and down the bike route with water and nutrition supplies, acting as a roving aid station. My support came in handy on a few occasions – correcting wrong turns and fixing a flat tire for someone with no repair kit. Perhaps the biggest benefit of having a support car and person for such a long ride is just the comfort in knowing a car is always nearby should the need arise.

The day of the race I awoke with everyone else at 4 a.m. and then cheered my butt off until nearly midnight. It was easy to see everyone on team Stoke Multisport cared deeply about their fellow teammates as they were constantly asking me how their friends were doing in the race. The run course has several spots where runners are heading in opposite directions so they were able to see each other. Each time one of the Stoke Multisport members would pass one another they would exchange high-fives and encouragement. The entire team, whether they finished in twelve hours or sixteen hours, waited for the final team member who finished a bit past 11 p.m.; a sixteen-plus-hour day, beating the event's famous midnight (17-hour) deadline. Imagine going to an epic event like IRONMAN, knowing your team members are ALL gathered at the finish line cheering you on. It's a wonderful feeling knowing you are not alone.

Just after midnight, several of us who were still standing celebrated the day's amazing accomplishments with a cold beer in the hotel bar. On the surface, it might look like just a weekend trip for a triathlon. Having been involved in several of these trips I know firsthand it goes so far beyond a casual weekend away. This will be a trip these athletes treasure for years to come. For me, I can tell you I made some new friendships that will be intact for a long time. I know this because of the many friends I have who say things like, "How long ago was it that we went down to Monterey for the Pacific Grove Triathlon with Team In Training? Eleven years? I can't believe it's been that long. That was such a great team!"

Eleven years from now the Stoke Multisport team will be fondly recalling the trip to Madison with that same smile I've shared with thousands of athletes.

Wildflower

I have had some starkly contrasting experiences at triathlon races and can absolutely tell you, races shared with friends make for a far more enjoyable experience. In 1996 I decided to do the Wildflower Triathlon in California. It was known as the Woodstock of triathlon; a giant party. It was also known as one of the toughest long course triathlons around (1.2-mile swim, 56-mile bike, 13.1-mile run). Everything I read about the iconic race made the point it was a MUST-do race.

Everyone camps at Wildflower (because it's in the middle of nowhere) so I figured I'd just spend the night in the rental car. After all, I was there to race and to test myself far more than to party, unlike many of the other participants. Plus, you may be surprised to learn I am an introvert so the thought of randomly joining a large group of strangers would not be something I'd be comfortable with, although I am envious of people who can easily strike up conversations and make friends. The introverts reading this can relate, I'm sure.

I had a horrible night of sleep as large groups of people were laughing and telling stories late into the night. The race itself went pretty well despite the less than stellar night of sleep. I vividly remember crossing the finish line and sitting on the grass alone. Not a single person to share my race with. Not a single person there to cheer me on during the race. Remember, this was before cell phones were common, so it was just me; no one to talk about the race with, no one to complain about the heat and the tough course, just me and my tired body. I remember looking around at all the other people sharing their stories of their race and having a good time. After about thirty minutes I packed up my stuff and left. I had never felt so lonely in the sport.

The Lavaman Triathlon

Fortunately, I've had many race experiences that were exactly the opposite of my Wildflower experience. This is perhaps one of the things I love most about Team In Training; having an entire team of people to share not just the race day but the entire weekend with. As I mentioned earlier, many of my friends have come through TNT. I've been incredibly fortunate to coach TNT teams for the Lavaman Triathlon on the Big Island of Hawaii. I've been to the race at least ten times and it's easily one of my favorite races.

How can you beat watching the sun rise over Mauna Kea while you set up your transition and get ready for the swim with the palm trees gently blowing in the wind and the temperature a beautiful 75 degrees? During the swim, you are likely to spot sea turtles and schools of colorful Hawaiian fish swimming in and out of the coral. Then you get to ride on hallowed ground - the Queen Ka'ahumanu Highway, affectionately known as The Queen K, the bike course for IRONMAN World Championships. After the bike, it's a challenging run through the resorts and out to the lava fields where you can really feel the heat and humidity. It's here where you get a small taste of how truly difficult IRONMAN in Hawaii is.

The Lavaman run ends on the beach with a picturesque backdrop of the amazingly blue ocean. After the race, athletes enjoy barbecue and free flowing kegs of beer from the Kona Brewing Company. Sitting under the palm trees on the beach sharing race stories while staring at the ocean and listening to the gentle waves roll in; does it get any better? It's a race like no other, that's for sure!

However, what really makes the Lavaman Triathlon special for me beyond the incredible location and race scenery is the friendships I've made during race weekends. There are opportunities for bonding in the few days before the race when the team swims in the ocean, and many athletes are experiencing their first-ever ocean swims.

I've spent time on the beach with a few athletes as they sat there sobbing, expressing their fears of the water, telling me about their traumatic experiences as a child. Patiently, we talked and waited, until eventually we waded out into the water and took just a few strokes before standing up to regroup - then a few more strokes. Feeling more comfortable we'd go a little further. Next thing you know, the very next day they are exiting the swim on race day, and as they come running up the beach they see me there waiting and cheering. At that moment, they become an incredible mix of all-out enthusiasm and uncontrollable crying. These are life-changing moments and I get goosebumps reliving them. Shared memories such as these create life-long friendships.

New in Town?

If you ever find yourself moving to a new city, one of the best things you can do for yourself is to find, and most importantly, show up for a group workout. Triathletes on average are a very welcoming bunch of people. However, it may also require you to come out of your shell, if you're an introvert. Show up, introduce yourself, allow yourself to be a little vulnerable by saying something like you are new to the area and you're not sure if this group is the right training group but you'd like to give it a try. It's amazing how when you let your guard down and show a little vulnerability, people will readily help you out and take you under their wing.

When I moved to Seattle a guy I worked with at the running store named Wade heard that I was doing all of my riding on the Burke-Gilman Trail, an old railroad line converted into a flat paved straight line. Wade took me on all kinds of different routes until I knew how to connect various loops and routes creating an entire catalogue of rides for me to choose from. If not for Wade, I might still just be riding on the "Burke" as we say in Seattle.

Speaking of connections, Wade and I also joined forces in 2000 to put in the first triathlon program for Team In Training in Seattle. We also worked together at Super Jock 'n Jill for eight years before opening our own running store together called Everyday Athlete in 2004. Perhaps if he'd never offered to take me riding, none of that would have ever happened. We'll never know, but I am glad it did.

My wife, Janine, and I moved to San Diego for a short time in 2003 and the first thing I did was reach out to Team In Training to see if they needed any coaches. Gurujan Dourson was the man I would need approval from. Coach Gurujan interviewed me, grilled me a little bit, then hired me as his assistant for the season. I had no idea that Janine and I would move back to Seattle within the year. I also had no idea that Coach Gurujan and I would meet up year after year in Hawaii for the Lavaman Triathlon when we were both coaching TNT; he in San Diego and I in Seattle. Coach Gurujan and I would spend hours tearing up the dance floor at the victory parties, both of us loving to dance, especially with our favorite dance partner, Tara V. Smith. Whenever we see each other we have the bond of the Lavaman Triathlon and of TNT. In fact, I was recently in San Diego for a conference and Coach Gurujan and I met up for coffee. Sure enough he asked, "How's my girl Tara doing?"

I knew in reaching out to TNT when moving to San Diego I would find people to make the transition easier, but I did not expect to make a lifelong friend. To this day, I'm still in contact with several people from my eight months in San Diego and as a side benefit I went on all kinds of great bike rides I might have never known existed.

You Never Know Who You Will Meet

Seemingly innocent connections affect not only the present but have the potential for future cosmic changes. My good friends Sarah and Marian, whom I met back in 2006 when they both signed up for the Pacific Crest Long Course Triathlon as part of Team In Training, are best friends and have been since that team. Neither has done a triathlon for several years but their friendship has transcended triathlon. They still run together, but now it's more for dinner parties and vacations. Sarah tells a funny story about going to a TNT recruitment event for the program and upon hearing how people in TNT often meet their future spouse or best friend, had to keep herself from gagging.

I was there to raise money for The Leukemia and Lymphoma Society and to race. I wasn't looking for friends. It just felt like they were trying to make this into some big life-changing, emotional event. But in the end it was, at least for me. When I started with the TNT team it didn't take long to realize that Marian and I were almost a perfect match in both biking and running, and we also ended up in the same lane at the pool. So we started training together. A lot. With that came long runs and long bike rides, which inevitably became long discussions about our daily lives, our relationships, what we were celebrating and what we were struggling with. And it became lots of head-to-head races, where we were competing with each other probably more than with anyone else. My experience had always been that friendship and competition don't go well together, but Marian grew up running track in an environment that was both supportive and competitive. She showed me how to be competitive in a really healthy way. I still try to kick her butt whenever I can - but if I can't, I celebrate along with her, then use it as motivation to go faster, longer, harder. So, in the end TNT was right, and I still laugh about it to this day.

Support Network

There is another very important characteristic to community, and that is support. If you want to achieve your dreams and goals, build yourself a community of people who will support you. Next time you are around a group of friends, tell them you want to do something new you've never done and are nervous about tackling. Perhaps you are worried you won't succeed or don't know where to begin. Allow yourself to be vulnerable. Watch what happens. Your friends will come up with all kinds of reasons you will absolutely be able to accomplish your goal and they'll remind you of your strengths. If you encounter the opposite reaction and they tell how you'll fail and what a fool you are to attempt such a thing, you need to find new friends! I'm absolutely dead serious. Do not surround yourself with people who will drag you down. Instead, seek out people who will encourage you, inspire you and cheer you on.

Jim Rohn said, "You are the average of the five people you spend the most time with." If you want to elevate your life in any area, figure out the five people you spend the most time with in that area and elevate your five. Find some people who emulate the skillset or personality of what you are seeking. If you want to become a faster triathlete, start training with people who are slightly faster than you. But don't pick people who are several levels above you as you'll either not be able to keep up with them or you'll end up injured very quickly.

All it Takes is one Person to Believe

I was incredibly fortunate to attend two of Dave Scott's Triathlon Certification courses for Team In Training. In 2001, at the Level I certification I heard him say, "No one cares how much you know until they know how much you care." Until I recently Googled it, I assumed that gem came straight from "The Man" himself. But I learned it's a quote from Theodore Roosevelt. Either way, I've carried that quote in my head ever since, always reminding myself that I first needed to create a connection with athletes that I coach before they would listen to what I had to teach about triathlon.

The support aspect of community is one of my most important jobs as a coach. So many times when I have an athlete who has never completed an Olympic distance triathlon and they have a lot of doubt as to whether they can accomplish this goal, I have to believe in them far more than they believe in themselves. I have to believe in them so much that it will allow them, just for a period of time, to suspend their self-doubt. Eventually their mindset shifts from, "I don't think I can do this." to, "Maybe I can do this." and then to, "I think I can do this." And finally, "I know I can do this!" Just one person believing in them allows each athlete to take the next step. This is so critical.

Then, as is so common, when they cross the finish line and their faces are completely lit up and I can hear in their voices how pumped up they are, I know they have become different people. Just as when I crossed the finish line of my first race. Naturally we ponder, "What else can I do?" We begin to wonder if we could go faster or farther. This new-found confidence allows us to begin to wonder what opportunities and challenges outside of triathlon are possible. The next journey begins.

From Impossible to I'm Possible

People ask me all the time why I keep coming back year after year to coach Team In Training and the answer is always the same; it's because of the people I meet and get to connect with. It's the relationships I forge. Kelly's story represents perfectly why I love coaching.

I went from running marathons, to running 5Ks, to hardly running at all, before a friend convinced me to train for my first Olympic-distance triathlon with Lance as our coach. For our first bike practice, I showed up wearing cotton scrubs (I work at a hospital) with my helmet cocked to one side. No judgment from Lance, only an enthusiastic pep talk that inspired me to bike two loops instead of one. Six months later I was held up by 15-hour travel delays on three standby connections flying from Seattle to Kona to compete in the Lavaman Triathlon. Meanwhile, Lance was assembling my bike for me the day before the race, in a crowded hotel ballroom with hundreds of my teammates, so I could start out fresh. Although I toppled over in the bike-to-run transition in that race, I was smiling - almost as big as Lance's grin as he watched us cross the finish line.

Later that summer, Lance invited us to consider a full distance triathlon. He assembled us for a lakeside talk. As the sun was setting, in moments of quiet introspection, I took in the magnitude of the commitment I was about to make. It would require a year of training, nine workouts a week (three of each sport), and long bike rides or bricks every Saturday for a year. And that's just the physical commitment. I put in the work and I listened to Lance, as he taught us how to replace calories during a marathon, to receive a water bottle handoff while in motion on our bikes, and to swim in churning water. He built up our mental fitness too, helping me find resilience when workouts didn't go well, trust in my preparation, and dig deep when my body was sore. Months into the season, one of my teammates told me that out of everyone on the team, he pegged me as least likely to finish. But Lance, by contrast, never once doubted me. As accomplished an athlete as Lance is, he celebrated our accomplishments with absolute pride and joy. He believed in us.

On race day, I was surrounded by uber-competitive triathletes jostling for position, yet I was the picture of calm because I knew I could do it. That feeling when you cross the finish line of IRONMAN for the first time is hard to put into words. I just know that Lance had an incredible impact on my fitness, my self-confidence, my willingness to try things that scare me, and my optimism that I can do anything if I set my mind to it. He taught me that anything is possible.

Kelly's story is one that I've come back to time and again over my coaching career because it reminds me just how important connection is. I specifically choose the quote from Kurt Vonnegut to begin this chapter because he said it well before the technological revolution and yet it seems to capture so eloquently our current state of being. Here we are as a society with our smartphones and social media where we are all "connected" and yet we've never been so disconnected from each other. We stare at our phone instead of making eye contact; text instead of talk. More than ever we need to create true connection with other humans. We need communities. The beautiful thing is that when we do create these communities and connections, we can create incredibly impactful relationships as well as lifelong memories. I've been very blessed in this regard as this next story reveals.

Reverend Run

I've been honored to be asked by two different couples to marry them. Not in the "moving-to-Utah-polygamy" kind of way but in the "I now pronounce you husband and wife" kind of way. It's a very humbling and an incredible honor to be asked to take on such a pivotal role in one of the most important days for two people. In 2014 my dear friends Kristen and Chris shocked me one day when they asked me to marry them.

My first thought was, "Why me?" Honestly, I couldn't imagine why they would ask me. I wasn't ordained or licensed to perform such a task. Other than being their good friend, I was baffled as to the reason. My second thought was, "Why me?" I am most definitely not comfortable being the center of attention or in the limelight and the thought of being front and center of the ceremony was paralyzing. The pressure of not completely ruining such a special day was very traumatic for me. I said yes, mostly because it seemed rude to decline. I'd have to suck it up and rise to the occasion.

The weeks leading up the wedding had me waking up in the middle of the night in a cold sweat having nightmares about opening my mouth only to have somehow lost my voice. One thing that helped take some of the pressure off was thinking to myself, "If I'm going to do this, then at least I'm going to have some fun with it and borrow the nickname *Reverend Run.* What the heck, I'm a runner and I grew up with Run-D.M.C. and Def Jam

Recordings so when it came to the wedding . . . just call me *Reverend Run*.

Two years after the wedding I still really didn't FULLY understand why Kristen and Chris chose me. Feeling anxious and somewhat vulnerable, I asked Kristen for a deeper answer than, "Because you really mean a lot to us." Reading her words in answer to that question has been one of the greatest gifts I've ever received. Kristen reminded me of several occasions when I played a significant role in her life; first as a triathlon coach through Team In Training, next as her boss when I gave her a job when the Great Recession hit, and then as an advisor when she took the leap to leave the safety of the corporate world for pursuing her passion of helping people through SOMA (integrated body work). Here's a portion of what Kristen shared with me about why she and Chris chose me.

SO . . . here are the reasons that we asked you to marry us: You are a person we both look up to in exponential ways. You are on top of your shit, you are driven and responsible, organized and thorough and incredibly generous with your time and energy. You are kind and accepting of people but you are able to provide a strong counsel without being "judgy" or critical, and that felt like what we both needed. We value your marriage and knew we'd value your guidance though our ceremony prep. You and Janine really acted as our marriage counselors in that process, whether you knew it or not, designing our ceremony with you two was a beautiful growth for us.

The reason I am telling this story is to remind all of us that we are never fully aware of the effect we have on the people around us. Sometimes people touch our lives in ways we can't imagine and sometimes we do the same for others. It reminds me of the famous line from the movie, *It's a Wonderful Life* from Clarence the Angel, "No man is a failure who has friends." Be your authentic self and do your best to add value to other people's lives and you'll impact people in ways you might never imagine.

Find Your Community

All of us are capable of achieving more than we allow ourselves to believe. When we find even one person to believe in us and support us it is often the difference-maker, allowing us to strive for and achieve things we once considered unreachable. Find your community of support and don't stop searching until you find your tribe. If you can't find one, create one. There are many people in the world who share your hopes, dreams, challenges and fears. Put yourself out there and allow others in. Doing so will change your life and you just might change the life of someone else in the process.

6

Coaching: The Difference that Makes the Difference

If you set a goal for yourself and are able to achieve it, you have won your race. Your goal can be to come in first, to improve your performance, or just to finish the race – it's up to you.

Dave Scott

Getting Where You Want to go, Only Faster

If you want to speed up your achievement curve, find someone who's been where you want to go; someone who's accomplished what you want to do; a mentor or a coach. Find someone who's already made many of the mistakes you'll want to avoid; someone you can turn to when you are stuck or in need of a pep talk.

The role of a coach serves two primary purposes - strategy and motivation. Granted, under each of these main purposes are a host of other responsibilities, however these are the two critical components to coaching. In fact, they are the two primary components to anything you want to achieve. You will need a plan, a road map, a direction, and a course of action. This does not mean you need to figure out every step of the way in advance, because usually the plan will need to change as you progress and move through your journey. There are hurdles, roadblocks, side roads, and all kinds of obstacles that will come your way and you'll need to adapt. No matter what though, you MUST begin! You must take action!

Most experts will tell you that "how" you'll get there is much less of a concern than the "why." If you have a strong enough why, you'll figure out the how. After all, where would we be if humans were only able to do things that had already been done?

"If you really want to do something, you'll find a way. If you don't, you'll find an excuse." – Jim Rohn

Strategy

Once you figure out what it is in life you want to set your compass toward, find someone to make your journey easier. Find someone who has already accomplished what you aim for. Their experience and knowledge will help you in countless and unforeseen ways.

Your coach is there to guide you and to help you set your course. He or she is there when you get off course and need to figure out the best way to get back on track. Your coach will also be able to tell you all the good things you are doing. He will encourage you when things are going well and help you correct course when you are a little off. Coaches have the experience and knowledge to get you where you want to go. One of the best parts of hiring a coach is that you don't have to research what needs to be done, or in what sequence and how often. You don't have to worry about the how and it simplifies the process of moving forward.

Don't forget, "coaches" and "mentors" are not limited to people you know or can hire. Books are still a fantastic way to learn how to do something. Of course, we have the internet, including YouTube to learn new skills. Regarding triathlon, finding a training schedule is easier than ever. The harder part these days might be evaluating the many free training plans, making it difficult to choose because too many options can be paralyzing.

When it comes to picking a training plan or following the plan your coach lays out for you, keep in mind the best training plan is the one you *do*. When it comes to triathlon it's still about fitness. If you do eighty-plus percent of a training plan, odds are you are going to have a fantastic race. If you do twenty percent of a training plan, odds are your race is going be really tough.

It's not the plan, it's the practice. It's the implementation of the plan. It's taking action. It's training and training consistently.

Accountability

Most of us will accomplish our goals more completely when we have someone to hold us accountable. I first noticed this in the personal training methods that are commonplace in gyms. At first the judgmental part of me thought people who hired personal trainers were just weak or lazy. Over time I began to realize all of us, myself included, need help at different times and in different areas to achieve the results we desire. People hire personal trainers mostly because they know they need motivation to work out and the trainer provides this motivation. This is not any different from hiring a triathlon coach, a business coach, a business consultant, a life coach, or any other expert. In fact, anytime someone hires another person to help them accomplish something, accountability is one of the biggest reasons for doing so. We humans are far more likely to do something when we pay for it and when we have other people holding us accountable.

The great news is you don't always have to pay for accountability. This is why weekly training workouts led by a local running store, group workouts and training partners can prove vital to success for so many people. When your friend is at the track waiting for you at 6 a.m., you go the track because you don't want to bail on your friend; you drag your butt out of bed even though you want to sleep. If you want to do an event and you know you need accountability, encourage one of your friends to join you on your journey. Your odds of completing the journey increase when you enlist a friend to join you. The two of you will hold each other accountable and encourage the other when one of you is down.

Who can you make a deal with to be each other's accountability partner? This works for triathlon as well as any area of your life you want to improve. You may have one accountability partner for swimming, and a different partner for biking, etc. Don't limit this idea to just your athletic life. If you are wanting to take your business to a new level, find someone who is looking to do the same. Share your goals and plans with each other and then meet regularly to keep each other on track. Provide each other with encouragement as well as feedback and suggestions. Not only will you will reach your goals faster, but you'll have someone to celebrate with!

A coach is the perfect person to provide accountability. You may not always meet in person with your coach, but when she gives you a training schedule, there are rewards and consequences. When you complete the schedule, you feel good about yourself and you may receive praise from the coach, which also makes you feel good. We're not that different from animals; praise does wonders. When you miss workouts, you know you have to tell your coach, which does not feel good. You don't want to let your coach down and often that motivates you to get your work done. Often the simple act of paying money for something motivates you to follow through. Hiring a coach can be proof to yourself that you are willing to invest in yourself!

I have a slogan that reads: *Race to train and train to race.* One of my secrets for training and racing for over twenty-three years is that I race to train and train to race. You're probably wondering what that means. If I don't have a race planned just far enough in the future, typically four to six months out, one that scares me just enough knowing if I slack on my training the race will absolutely suck and be painful, then it's far too easy for me to skip exercise altogether. I can take weeks off when there is no race on my horizon. When I do this, the rest of my life quickly deteriorates. I get cranky because I'm not exercising. How I feel about myself as a person lessens, how I relate to other people deteriorates. Thankfully I've learned over time that I am a much better person when I exercise.

For those reasons, I put races on my calendar to motivate myself to train because I know that I live a higher quality of life because of it. I also train so that when the race comes around I'm not miserable hating every minute of it, as so often happens when the preparation is not adequate. I train so I can have my best performance possible given my current situation. I train because I know the feeling of having a great race. I love that feeling, knowing all the training came together just right and I crushed it. It's one of the times when I feel the most alive; knowing I reached my full potential.

Motivation

You don't fail because you don't know how to do something. Maybe there is temporary failure. however these are really just learning experiences and opportunities. You fail because you give up, you stop trying. Michael Jordan, one of the most competitive athletes of all time, NCAA Champion with the University of North Carolina in 1982, six-time NBA Champion with the Chicago Bulls in 1991, 1992, 1993, 1996, 1997 and 1998, has a quote that is worth repeating, "I've missed more than nine thousand shots in my career. I've lost almost three hundred games. Twenty-six times, I've been trusted to take the game-winning shot and missed. I've failed over and over and over again in my life. And that is why I succeed." Thomas Edison, one of the greatest inventors of all time is famously quoted as saying, "I have not failed, I've just found ten thousand ways that won't work."

Even when you truly don't know how to do something, you can learn from others. Absolutely there are things that have truly never been accomplished, but most of what you seek has been accomplished many times over. The veterans, the experts, the mentors, and the coaches are out there. The harder part of the equation is not figuring out how to do something, but providing yourself with the motivation and the "why" behind your aspirations.

Here's the great news: you can not only strengthen your "why" but you can also create your own motivation. When you sign up for a race, join a training group or class, hire a coach, or set a goal, you are creating motivation for yourself. It is a mind shift in setting a higher goal.

Think back to the quote from Tony Robbins at the beginning of Chapter 1: "People are not lazy. They simply have impotent goals – that is goals that do not inspire them." Maybe like me, all you really need is a goal big enough to create such massive inspiration that it will allow you to take massive action. I don't know your situation. Things could be fantastic in all areas of your life except one. Maybe things are "fine" but you don't feel alive. One question I would ask, "Are your goals inspiring to you?"

Would you like to strengthen your motivation right now? Pick a goal or something that you are either working toward right now or want to achieve in the future. Take out a journal or notebook. Answer the following questions:

- What are my reasons for wanting this?

- What will it mean to my life when I achieve my goal?

- What will it cost me if I do not achieve my goal?

- How will achieving this goal impact other people in my life both negatively and positively?

- Who can I turn to for advice?

- What books can I read on this topic? What podcasts can I listen to?

- What question(s) can I ask myself that will inspire me to reach this goal?

- Who do I need to become, what skills do I need to learn, what thoughts do I need to think, to become the person who can achieve this goal?

- What one characteristic best symbolizes the person I need to be to achieve my goal?

- How can I remind myself of this characteristic multiple times throughout the day?

- Can I set an alarm in my phone to pop up every day labeled with this characteristic? Can I post a note on my bathroom mirror? Can I carry around this word in my pocket on the back of a business card?

- What is the best way for me to live this characteristic?

- What does success mean to me?

If you are waiting for and relying on other people and events to provide your motivation, then you are missing out on your best life. You must take ownership of *your* motivation.

That being said, I challenge myself to motivate the athletes I coach. Ultimately, I feel it is up to them to claim ownership but I also believe that as their coach it is my responsibility to do my best to understand them, challenge them when needed, encourage them when needed, and inspire them to the best of my ability.

The Mental Aspect

Too often people downplay the mental aspect of achievement. Whether in sport or life the mind makes the ultimate difference. Too often, people make the mistake of saying and thinking, "Just tell me what to do," as if that's all there is to it. You can DO all the necessary steps but if your mind is fighting against you then you are either not going to reach your goals or you will find a way to sabotage yourself before you reach those goals.

If you enjoy what you do, you will get there much quicker and enjoy the process a lot more. I like to tell the athletes I coach, "Since neither of us are going to become professional triathletes we might as well enjoy what we are doing, otherwise what's the point?" Triathlon should be something that enhances and complements our lives; it should not BE our lives.

It's important to strengthen the mind as it has such an enormous impact on our physical performance. Think about Roger Bannister breaking the four-minute mile. It was thought to be impossible. Until he did it. Shortly after, fifty-six days in fact, John Landy broke four minutes. Now high school runners break four minutes for the mile every year and nobody thinks much of it. The impossible becomes possible and then it becomes routine. It all starts with the mind.

Our mind is our greatest asset and all we have to do is tap into its power.

Jenn

Recently I had the opportunity to work with an athlete who came to me commenting that she wasn't sure if she wanted to continue in the sport and that she no longer enjoyed it. Here's Jenn's story in her words:

Well, when I came to Lance, it was after what I'd call a 'bad breakup' with another coach. Let me tell you, all coaches are not the same. The last coach broke me, not only physically, but even worse, mentally.

Lance started coaching me with very little time before my big race. I felt like before we ever approached the physical part of the sport, he dealt with the mental. He helped me find the love of why I was doing what I was doing, he helped me find that drive to push through the hard training days and days where I lacked motivation. He got me back on track.

With less than three months, I not only completed IRONMAN, but I set a PR (personal record). The swim was the biggest physical coaching change we made. With two group sessions and one one-on-one session, I took over seven minutes off my IRONMAN triathlon swim time. That is one-hundred percent because of the little tweaks Lance made with my swim technique.

I look forward to seeing what's in store for me and improvements I will continue to make not just in the swim, bike, and run, but also in the ever-so-overlooked fourth part of triathlon: The mental leg.

A big part of the reason that Jenn set her IRONMAN race PR was because of the large volume of training that she had done prior to our working together. The training that made her stronger eventually went too far to the point of causing injury. Furthermore, the guilt associated with possibly missing a workout even though she was deeply fatigued and had a shoulder injury led to mental anguish. This was a recipe for disaster. Immediately upon working together we reduced her training volume by nearly forty percent and she responded very well physically, and not surprisingly, began to enjoy working out again.

Her swim time improved because we improved the mechanics of her swim stroke and made it more efficient, allowing her to swim faster with the same effort. Between the large amount of work she had already completed and the improvement to her swimming, she was in a position to have a great race. However, without turning around the mental aspect, none of that would have mattered.

I firmly believe had we not been able to turn around her mental state there is a very high likelihood she never would have made it to the start line of her race. It's difficult to sustain an activity when you dread it. And even if Jenn had been able to push on and make the start line of the race I doubt she would have set a PR because she would not have been at her best mentally.

There is a key takeaway for you in Jenn's story. Connect with the aspects of your sports, your hobbies and, yes, even your job - that you love, that you enjoy, and that bring pleasure to your life. Focus on those aspects and you'll find yourself achieving more in these areas.

Jedi Mind Tricks

One of my favorite things about coaching is showing athletes how triathlon transfers to other areas in their lives, improving those areas. When you commit to a goal like completing an event, whether it's a Sprint triathlon or a full distance triathlon, if that distance is something you've never done and is intimidating to you; it's going to take commitment. Likewise, if you have already completed this distance and now are attempting to go faster, that too is going to take commitment on your part. Both are going to test you and make you question how badly you want it. They are going to require you to do some soul searching and go deep within yourself to see if you can answer the call and rise above your insecurities and self-doubt. The training takes place over several months and creates growth within the athlete. However, it is on race day where the changes an athlete has gone through explode with full force.

From the time waiting in the pre-dawn hours until the starting gun goes off to when you cross the finish line, you emerge a different person. It's like taking the transformation of a caterpillar to a butterfly and reducing it to one day. The stage for metamorphism has been taking shape all through the training and the buildup to the race, but in the race, in the heat of the moment, feelings are magnified. The heightened state of being is why the race experience feels so powerful. When you feel scared you become terrified. Anxiousness can easily escalate into a panic attack. Feelings of joy become elation. The pride of accomplishment becomes life changing. Additionally, it's the range of emotions that athletes go through on race day that leads to such an epic accumulation and out-pouring of emotion that is on display at the finish line.

It's entirely common to witness people crying as they cross the finish line. There are also instances of jubilation, primal screams; fist pumping and high fiving. Watching the athletes I've coached cross the finish line regardless of race distance, seeing the smiles on their faces, hearing the excitement in their voices, and noticing how they carry themselves in a new way are all signs they are different, more confident people.

It's always my hope they will use their race experiences as encouragement to tackle things they have always wanted to do in other areas of life. That by doing a triathlon they will learn they are indeed capable of achieving more than they believed and they will take that newfound confidence into other areas of their lives. I've been very fortunate to have hundreds of people tell me they've experienced this exact feeling. Each time I hear a story of how an athlete took their new-found confidence gained from a race and applied that confidence to tackle another seemingly unconnected area of their life, I smile and think to myself, "Jedi mind trick."

Kelsey

This crossover effect is why I asked Kelsey to write the foreword for my book. Think about being in your early twenties and having your dad, with whom you are very close, taken by cancer. As Kelsey wrote, for her it was paralyzing. She needed movement to reinvigorate her passion for living, to move forward with her life. Between the fundraising she did to benefit The Leukemia and Lymphoma Society in her dad's honor and the triathlon training, she emerged from the race different than when she began. I too remember that first Skype call and Kelsey asking me if I thought she really could complete an Olympic Distance Triathlon; hearing the doubt in her question. More accurately, hearing the doubt in herself.

Now, it could have been any number of activities that helped Kelsey process her grief, but it was triathlon.

The night before the Lavaman Triathlon at the Team In Training Inspiration Dinner, Kelsey gave the most beautiful speech and tribute to her father in front of more than five hundred people. It's in those moments when I am most proud to be a triathlon coach because it's those moments that transcend the sport. I remember Kelsey's mom asked me to take her phone to record a video of the speech as she knew she'd be too emotional to keep a steady hand. I gladly obliged and had to work hard to keep the phone steady myself as I fought back the tears.

Until that point, I had no idea if Kelsey's participation in our team and/or my coaching had any impact at all on her life, but it didn't matter. It was more than enough for me to share the experience with her and to support her to the best of my ability. To know now that I played a role in helping such an incredible person heal an aching heart ranks among my greatest accomplishments in my time as a coach.

Go for it!

I cannot encourage you enough to put your fear aside and truly go for it. If you are debating with yourself about taking the plunge, find a mentor. Find someone to encourage you. A mentor can guide you through the process. A mentor can help you find the confidence to take that needed first step. Find someone to bounce ideas off of, workouts and training plans to discuss. Find someone who's already accomplished what you want to accomplish so they can speed up your process and make it smoother for you. Life is for living. Put yourself out there. Take a risk. Live. But don't just live . . .

7

Live Big

The biggest adventure you can ever take is to live the life of your dreams.

Oprah Winfrey

Three Books

As I mentioned in Chapter 3, my friend Allison recommended that I read three books. These books dramatically changed the forward trajectory of my life. It was less than six months prior to summoning the courage to begin writing this book that I read the three books Allison recommended. Here again are the three books that blew my mind and kicked off a whirlwind inside my brain.

- *The Millionaire Messenger: Make a Difference and a Fortune Sharing Your Advice* by Brendon Burchard.

- *The Miracle Morning: The Not-So-Obvious Secret Guaranteed to Transform Your Life (Before 8AM)* by Hal Elrod.

- *The Big Leap: Conquer Your Hidden Fear and Take Life to the Next Level* by Gay Hendricks.

Brendon Burchard and Hal Elrod have both impacted my life from so many angles – books, podcasts, online courses, and weekend conferences. There is little doubt on how much influence they've had on my transformation. I would not be the person I've grown to become over the past year and a half had I not been introduced to the work of Brendon and Hal. With all of that said, *The Big Leap* is the book that shook me to my core and exposed me to the idea that I've been living small, afraid to live to my potential.

My Big Leap

Gay Hendricks talks about his "Upper Limit Theory" and how as we approach it, we begin to sabotage our success. He says there are four main reasons people sabotage themselves. As I was reading them, none of the first three resonated with me. If I strained, two of them kind of made sense, but nothing earth shattering. I was beginning to think this book just wasn't for me when I read number four. My heart began pounding in my chest; it went up at least twenty beats per minute and I had goosebumps on my forearms. I was dazed. Number four was not wanting to stand out among your peers and instead choosing to live small. I felt like the author had written that section just for me. I was overcome with sadness that I had chosen to live a life that was below what I was capable of and I knew it. At my core, I knew it. Even as I write this I am part saddened, part pissed off, and part motivated as hell to chart a new course.

I recalled several episodes from my childhood where I chose to do less than my best for fear of standing out and outshining my peers. I vividly remember purposely missing two questions on a test as a high school senior because I did not want to be one of only two people who got one-hundred percent correct. It was one of those rare times when I, without question, knew every answer.

Just the week before, several people in the class were complaining about how hard the recent test was. The teacher said something like, "If it was so hard, why did two people get every question correct?" I was one of the two people. I went to a small high school and my closest friends were in the "jock" crowd and not the "nerd" crowd. The students in the class, mostly led by my friends, began asking the "smart" kids if they were the ones who got one-hundred percent correct. The purpose of the questioning was to mock them for being "smart." It's the same scenario that plays out across the country and throughout the decades. I denied that I was one of those people and gratefully the teacher did not "out" me. The following week we had a test in a different subject and I knew every answer. After completing the test, I went back through it and changed two of my answers to wrong answers. When the test was returned to me, sure enough, the only two questions I missed were the ones I purposely changed.

Academics came easier to me than most people, I must admit. Having a brother just a couple of years older helped me learn subjects easier and sooner as a kid, at least that is what my mom tells me. There's no question I did not strive to reach my full potential. Because I made the decision to miss some test questions and live small, it felt like a little of my soul died. Looking back, I can take this story in stride, but it's also very sad and even pathetic on some level.

I have several similar stories about how I chose to live small and be less than my best. Some are too painful to tell, but I think you get the point. I want to reach back in time and tell the eight-year-old me, and the seventeen-year-old me how important it is to not hold myself back. I want to tell my younger self how much these seemingly temporary decisions will haunt my future self. I want to go back in time and be this kid's greatest cheerleader.

There has been at least one positive thing to come out of this experience. One of my greatest attributes as a coach is that I constantly believe in my athletes more than they believe in themselves. I always search for the positive in their struggles or disappointments and try my best to help them see the bigger picture. Writing this book helped me realize I am this way precisely because it's what I wanted growing up. I wanted the person in my corner unconditionally. I've become that for the athletes I coach.

It's not uncommon for people to sabotage themselves, and if you read *The Big Leap* you just might agree it's unfortunately entirely too common. You might even discover why you hold yourself back. Either way, from the moment I read those words they made my heart race. I decided I was done living small. From that point on, even if I failed, I would give it my all. I would do my best to LIVE BIG! Live Big would become my new mantra.

It's a very bold thing to declare that you are going to intentionally live your life to its fullest.

Now What?

Easier said than done, right? Where to begin? I knew I needed to embark on a new career as the world of brick and mortar retail had been steadily shifting toward an online culture. I knew I wanted to somehow positively impact other people's lives. It's what I've always felt I was doing by helping my customers in the twenty-three years I worked in the Run Specialty business; helping people find the right running shoes, apparel, and accessories for their endurance adventures. Sadly, the world of retail began to change, customers began to change, and the interactions began to change. It became a world of, "I can get that cheaper on the internet." Customers, not all but a lot, no longer valued the opinion of someone with years of experience; instead it became, "Well, according to the reviews online . . . ." I knew retail was no longer my path forward. If I'm honest, I was scared and frightened of an unknown future.

As I have taken more notice of other people and their lives it seems there is an all-too-common feeling of not knowing what to do with our lives. I certainly wasn't the only one to feel "lost." The main difference, it seemed to me, was that I took action. I didn't sit around hoping things would get better and hoping things would somehow work out.

As I read the books I've mentioned, along with countless others, I've challenged myself to not only learn new ideas but forced myself to take action. I asked myself hard questions and journaled about the answers. I've done lots of things that were not easy to do or even enjoyable, but I've also become a stronger person for having done them.

Self-Sponsored Terror

One of the most challenging things I've done is to record coaching videos and post them on social media for the world to see and possibly mock. If it doesn't sound hard to you, pick a topic and record yourself teaching this subject. Then post it! Maybe you'll be a natural and great for you! But chances are the self-criticism and self-evaluations will come out full force. I know for me, it was one of the most challenging things I've ever done.

I remember the first one I did, which I can laugh at now. I was sitting at my kitchen table staring into my iPad and I was sweating profusely. The negative chatter in my head was at full throttle. "Was I really going to do this? I suck. I can't even get through one sentence without stumbling. Is the lighting any good? Will anyone watch this? Will they die of laughter? Why am I doing this? Is it really necessary?" I did several takes and it took me almost an hour to record five minutes. It took another forty-five minutes or so to save, edit, and upload to YouTube. It took one gigantic breath and a serious leap of faith to post a link on my Facebook page. Thankfully it's gotten easier and I no longer break out in a cold sweat.

Reprogramming My Subconscious

As is so often the case for all of us, the biggest hurdle to overcome is us. We get in our own way. We stop ourselves before we even begin. We talk ourselves out of taking the risk. We often don't even realize our subconscious is the saboteur of living our best life. And if we do, we either don't know what to do or are too afraid to face our demons.

What I needed to work on was feeling good about charging a price for my services so I could create a career helping people; so I could make my difference in the world. Thankfully I was introduced to people I've mentioned throughout this book, who've really helped me to understand the value I have to offer people. Additionally, I've learned it's completely acceptable for me to charge for my coaching services and knowledge.

In fact, if I didn't charge what my services are worth I would find myself needing to find a "job" to pay my bills. That job would then take up most of my time which would mean I no longer had the time or energy to help the people I wanted to help. Ironically, not charging people for my services would mean I'd end up helping far fewer people, not to mention I might abandon the idea altogether.

So, I set about learning how and what I needed to do in order to offer my coaching services to the world. I did a deep dive into my thoughts and beliefs about myself and I confronted them, wrestled with them, pleaded and argued until I could say with confidence, "I am worth it." It wasn't easy and it took many months of determination and perseverance to be able to say those four words, but man was it worth the effort!

The Embodiment of Living Authentically

In chapter 4 I briefly mentioned the Best Year Ever (Blueprint) event. I was aware of this event since early 2016 but I didn't feel I could afford to go financially. Thankfully my good friend K.T. had signed up for the event and told me that if I joined her not only could I get a reduced price with the "bring a friend" discount, but she would pay for the hotel and I could crash in her room at no charge. I still had the mindset that I could not afford it. Then one day I had the idea that if I used some credit card points I could get a free plane ticket to San Diego. Now all of a sudden, it was beginning to seem financially possible. With a great deal of apprehension and nervousness, I said yes and committed to going with K.T. to the event. I can tell you it was one of the best decisions of my life.

I got my money's worth in the first five minutes of the two-day conference. Talk about an outstanding Return on Investment! Ever since reading *The Big Leap* I've been focusing on how to get out of my own way and how to summon the courage to live big; to really stop holding myself back. At the very beginning of the event, Jon Bergoff, the emcee, brought up on stage an incredibly energetic woman to lead us in some movement to boost the energy in the room. It was a combination of stretching, yoga, and dancing all set to pulsing music. There were over four hundred people in the room and she was leading everyone through a series of dance moves, all with nonverbal cues. All eyes in the room were locked on her. She was incredibly energetic and fully alive; practically mesmerizing. She was the absolute embodiment of what it meant to live fully present and not hold back. Right then, I had my role model of how I needed to move forward. Now, when I make my coaching videos, I take a moment to recall being in that room and not holding back. It's was a transformative experience for me.

At the first break in the conference, I did something I would have been previously too shy to do. I went up to her and introduced myself, "Hi, I'm Lance Carter." "Hi, I'm Andrea Riggs." I told her what a powerful experience it was for me to see her lead the entire room while it was obvious she was not the least bit self-conscious. We talked about what it meant to live unafraid to make mistakes and to risk looking foolish. She told me that my compliment made her day and she instantly led me over to the professional video and film crew to record a video testimonial for her.

What I learned in that moment is how important it is to live fully, not hold back, and let out all of the greatness we hold inside. Take a minute and think about who we are attracted to, who we want to follow and learn from. Is it the people who are reserved and shy or is it the people who are living big and bold; living as their authentic selves? It's the people who are passionately expressing themselves; the people who are excited and exciting. The people who are inspired and inspiring; those are the people who capture our hearts and minds. I recognized in that moment if I am to achieve my full potential I need to emulate Andrea. I need to stop holding back, let my true light shine and get out of my own way. My takeaway from Andrea was in perfect alignment with what I learned from *The Big Leap*; not wanting to outshine my peers.

It was time I began a new chapter in my life. It was time I made different choices. It was time I chose to live as my authentic self.

See Yourself Through Someone Else's Eyes

This is one of my favorite exercises. Think about some of your dear friends or people you greatly admire. Think about how you would describe them. Chances are you will list all the attributes you think are great about that person, such as their strengths and fantastic accomplishments. You'll either neglect or overlook their "flaws" or perceived weaknesses. Yet, if this same person were to describe themselves, their personal assessment would come back very different than yours. They would list more of their weaknesses and talk about all the things they have not accomplished or failed to do in the past.

The same thing would happen if you had someone who admires or looks up to you describe you. You would hear or read their version of you and you would instantly bring up your own deficiencies and shortcomings, and probably wonder how it's possible they see you this way. Meanwhile, they are wondering how you *don't* see yourself as they see you. Don't believe me? Try it. Ask someone who thinks you're wonderful, and comments how fantastic or talented you are. Ask them to describe you. Then listen or read their words and notice what comes up for you. Take it a step further and describe how you see them and then listen how they respond to your praise.

What's the point? The point is to see YOU through someone else's eyes; to allow yourself to see your talents, strengths, and value you bring to the world and other people. Next, and even more importantly, allow yourself to live as this person described by your friend. Allow yourself to go through your days believing you are the amazing person your biggest fans say you are. It doesn't mean that you abandon humility and become a self-serving narcissist. It just means that you allow yourself to live in and through your best self.

I believe in practicing what I preach so I challenged myself to do this same exercise. Back in September and October of 2016, over four weeks I was on the sidelines cheering on and supporting over seventy triathletes in three different IRONMAN races. After the third one, I challenged myself to journal about this idea of seeing myself through the eyes of these athletes. I filled several pages describing "Coach Lance" from their perspective. I wrote down the compliments they paid me and even allowed myself to expand on how I impacted their life. It was an incredibly powerful experience. My energy and self-belief were at an all-time high. It was the proverbial, "If I could bottle this feeling and sell it, I would be a millionaire."

The Choice is Yours

I made those videos, I did the work reprogramming my subconscious, I wrote blog posts, and created new coaching content because I needed to. I needed to do these things or else I would have remained stuck in my same patterns. I needed to move through and beyond my fear and self-limitation. I knew if I was going to live to my full potential, if I was going to **Live Big**, then I would have to walk through the fire.

If I am going to declare my life's purpose of empowering people to live more fulfilled lives through exercise and mindset elevation then I too need to challenge myself. I need to lead by example. I need to boldly state YES, I AM CAPABLE OF MORE!

I've created a 30-Day Challenge for you in a special bonus chapter. It's barely going to take a few minutes of your time each day, but I believe you will find, just like I did, that you end up becoming happier, more energized, more grateful, and living a life excited about your tomorrows.

My greatest hope for this book is that it inspires YOU to take action, go after YOUR dreams, and create a life of your dreams.

YOU ARE CAPABLE OF MORE!

Bonus Chapter

30-Day Challenge

I've spent a great deal of time reflecting on how I turned my mindset around, which has turned my life around. You can download all the worksheets for free at my website, LanceCarterCoaching.com/LEARN

Ready to take charge of your life? Ready to elevate your mindset? Ready to Live Big?

Day 1

Before going to bed, think of a few things you are looking forward to tomorrow. I like to pick at least three. They don't have to be grand things; they can be small enjoyments. Simple things like going for a run, meeting a friend for coffee, spending ten minutes meditating, reading one chapter from a book, and so forth.

If you can't think of anything that excites you about tomorrow, then it's a perfect opportunity to create some. Maybe you haven't spoken to a friend in too long so you make it a priority to call them tomorrow. Do you have a favorite lunch spot? Put it on your list. Do you have a favorite dinner? Make it. What brings you joy? Schedule it!

Don't forget, you can use the worksheets I've created for you at LanceCarterCoaching.com/LEARN

Day 2

Toward the end of your day, reflect on your day and give it a rating. I like to use a scale of 1 to 10 with 10 being an excellent day. You can use any rating system you choose.

Give your day a rating and then write down WHY you rated it as you did. The reason for this is that you will very soon figure out the events and people that help you live more enjoyable days and this practice will make painfully obvious the events and people that drag you down. You will become motivated to have your future days include more of the things and people that elevate your experience.

Day 3

Do five minutes of relaxing and deep breathing or try a five-minute guided meditation. Do a Google search on "5-minute guided meditation" and you'll get several options. Pick one that calls to you and give it a try.

Ideally, you'd do this (five minutes of relaxation or meditation) BEFORE turning on your phone or checking email. I took an online course from Oprah's "OWN Life Classes" taught by Brendon Burchard called, "Your Next Bold Move" and would highly recommend it! One of the best tips in the course was to avoid turning on your smartphone or checking email first thing upon waking up because when you do it's set your day up in total reaction mode.

Begin your day with either Intention or Reaction – the choice is yours. Checking your phone and email first thing in the morning sets up your day and your life in a reactionary state of mind instead of living your life with intention. I can tell from personal experience that when I incorporated this as part of my morning routine my brain felt like it had a lot more space and I went through my days more calm and less agitated. I will also tell you it's challenging, at first, to avoid going straight for your phone.

Can't meditate first thing in the morning? Pick a time in your day when you have five minutes to spare. Recently, in an interview I heard Tony Robbins say, "If you don't have ten minutes, you don't have a life." I laughed when I heard this as I've been preaching for nearly two years the enormous benefits of doing ten minutes of strength training each day. I laughed because of all the people who tell me they are so busy they don't have ten minutes in their day to do strength training, stretching, reading, meditating, etc. Meanwhile the average American watches over four hours of TV per day. Even if you only watch one hour of TV a day, you absolutely have ten minutes to spare. If your first response is that you don't have five minutes to spare, then you desperately need this 30-day challenge.

Day 4

MORNING ROUTINE

1. Begin your day by NOT turning on your phone to check for emails, calls, or to check social media.

2. Do another guided five-minute meditation or spend five minutes relaxing your body and mind while breathing deeply.

3. Write down at least one positive statement about yourself. Feel free to fill up the entire section for "Positive Journaling" found in the worksheets I've prepared for you.

EVENING ROUTINE

1. How would you rate today and why?

2. What are you excited about/looking forward to tomorrow?

Day 5

MORNING ROUTINE

1. Avoid turning on your phone until you've completed your morning routine.

2. Three Modified Sun Salutations. Here is a video by my friend Jennifer MacNiven, a yoga instructor and brilliant photographer to lead you through three Sun Salutations you can view at LanceCarterCoaching.com/LEARN. ALWAYS MAKE SURE YOU ARE CLEARED BY A PHYSICIAN BEFORE BEGINNING ANY EXERCISE PROGRAM.

3. Five minutes of meditation.

4. Positive Journaling. Can you strengthen what you wrote down yesterday? Think about the Bridge Statements I wrote about in Chapter 2. Notice what comes up for you. Are you uncovering limiting beliefs that you need to challenge?

EVENING ROUTINE

1. How would you rate today and why?

2. What are you excited about/looking forward to tomorrow?

Day 6

MORNING ROUTINE

1. Avoid turning on your phone until you've completed your morning routine.

2. Three Modified Sun Salutations. My friend Jennifer MacNiven has a video you can find at LanceCarterCoaching.com/LEARN that leads you through three Sun Salutations.

3. Five minutes of meditation.

4. Positive Journaling.

EVENING ROUTINE

1. Write down three things you are grateful for. Don't over-complicate this. If you are having a hard time identifying what you are grateful for ask yourself what you'd miss if it were suddenly taken from you.

2. How would you rate today and why?

3. What are you excited about/looking forward to tomorrow?

Day 7

Repeat Day 6. Repetition is the key to developing a successful daily routine.

Day 8

MORNING ROUTINE

1. Avoid turning on your phone until you've completed your morning routine.

2. Three Modified Sun Salutations.

3. Five minutes of meditation.

4. Positive Journaling.

EVENING ROUTINE

1. What are you grateful for?

2. Celebrate your accomplishments. What did you do well today that you can celebrate? Again, don't overcomplicate this and think you can only celebrate grand accomplishments. Maybe you were simply kind to the person who took your lunch order. Maybe you complimented a person and brought a smile to their face. Maybe you went swimming when you wanted to go home to your couch and TV.

3. How would you rate today and why?

4. What are you excited about/looking forward to tomorrow?

Day 9

Repeat Day 8. Are you noticing that you are beginning to feel a little more excited for each day or living with a little more energy?

Day 10

MORNING ROUTINE

1. Avoid turning on your phone until you've completed your morning routine.

2. Three Modified Sun Salutations.

3. Five minutes of exercise. If you have ten minutes, even better. Do some gentle stretching or yoga. Go for a brisk walk or do some calisthenics. I have created several ten-minute strength sessions you can try which are also found at LanceCarterCoaching.com/LEARN. ALWAYS MAKE SURE YOU ARE CLEARED BY A PHYSICIAN BEFORE BEGINNING ANY EXERCISE PROGRAM.

4. 5 minutes of meditation.

5. Positive Journaling.

EVENING ROUTINE

1. What are you grateful for?

2. Celebrate your accomplishments.

3. How would you rate today and why?

4. What are you excited about / looking forward to tomorrow?

Day 11

Repeat Day 10. If you've completed every day give yourself a big compliment. It's not uncommon to miss a day here or there. Hopefully you are noticing that the days you do these exercises are more fulfilling and it inspires you to want to make them a part of your everyday life.

Day 12

MORNING ROUTINE

1. Avoid turning on your phone until you've completed your morning routine.

2. Three Modified Sun Salutations.

3. Five or ten minutes of exercise.

4. Five minutes of meditation.

5. Write down your answers to the following questions:

- How do I want to show up in the world?

- What could my life look like such that I would feel fully alive?

- Who do I need to become to live this life I want to create?

- What characteristics do I need embody to live into this vision for myself?

6. Write down three attributes or characteristics of who you want to be/how you want to show up in the world. Carry those words around with you today.

7. Positive Journaling.

EVENING ROUTINE

1. What are you grateful for?

2. Celebrate your accomplishments.

3. How would you rate today and why?

4. What are you excited about/looking forward to tomorrow?

Day 13

Repeat Day 12. If you are still reading, then it most likely means that you are benefitting from this 30-Day Challenge. Share it with someone. Tell a friend. Share on social media. Spread the message and spread the love!

Day 14

MORNING ROUTINE

1. Avoid turning on your phone until you've completed your morning routine.

2. Three Modified Sun Salutations.

3. Five or ten minutes of exercise.

4. Five minutes of meditation.

5. How do you want to show up in the world?

6. Positive Journaling.

7. Create an Affirmation.

EVENING ROUTINE

1. What are you grateful for?

2. Celebrate your accomplishments.

3. How would you rate today and why?

4. What are you excited about/looking forward to tomorrow?

Days 15 and 16

Repeat Day 14. Excellent job! You're past two weeks and beginning to create your daily routine.

Day 17

MORNING ROUTINE

1. Avoid turning on your phone until you've completed your morning routine.

2. Three Modified Sun Salutations.

3. Five or ten minutes of exercise.

4. Five minutes of meditation.

5. How do you want to show up in the world?

6. What are you blessed to do? This may seem like an odd question, but think of all the things we complain about. I used to always say, "I have to run today" and then I spent nine months in physical therapy healing a running injury. Now I say, "I get to run today." Think about things you may complain about. Maybe it's your work, maybe it's your spouse or children. Now consider how you'd feel if those things were taken away. When the Great Recession hit, many people who complained about their "lousy" job were suddenly realizing that it was better than being out of work. Many people who lost their houses realized that having house chores was better than moving in with friends or relatives because their house was foreclosed on. It's a matter of perspective. In the United States we take clean water for granted while other people in the world have to walk miles to get clean water to drink. We take so much for granted. Take a little time to remind yourself of all that you are blessed to have and to do.

7. Positive Journaling.

8. Write down your affirmation(s).

EVENING ROUTINE

1. What are you grateful for?

2. Celebrate your accomplishments.

3. How would you rate today and why?

4. What are you excited about/looking forward to tomorrow?

Days 18 and 19

Repeat Day 17. By now you are beginning to identify the aspects of this challenge that are adding value to your life and you may be finding some that don't resonate with you as much. That's okay, everyone is different. You may also be noticing there are some activities that may not be your favorites or come easy to you but that you also recognize are important to your growth. Absolutely make a daily ritual of the concepts that add value to your life and don't shy away from the concepts that you know you need.

Day 20

MORNING ROUTINE

1. Avoid turning on your phone until you've completed your morning routine.

2. Three Modified Sun Salutations.

3. Five or ten minutes of exercise.

4. Five minutes of meditation.

5. Connect with your bigger vision. What are a few of your grandest dreams? What do you want to accomplish in your life? What grand vacation do

you want to take? Write these down. Allow yourself to dream. Stoke your ambition so that you can bring more meaning to each day of your life!

6. How do you want to show up in the world?

7. What are you blessed to do?

8. Positive Journaling.

9. Write down your affirmation(s).

EVENING ROUTINE

1. What are you grateful for?

2. Celebrate your accomplishments.

3. How would you rate today and why?

4. What are you excited about/looking forward to tomorrow?

Days 21 and 22

Repeat Day 20. Continue to connect with your bigger vision and allow yourself to feel the fire of passion. Do you really want to go through life getting from one day to the next just to do it all over again like you're stuck in the movie *Groundhog Day*? Or do you want to take charge of your life and create your reality so you can live your best life? You wouldn't have read this book or taken this challenge if you wanted to resign to a dreary day to day existence. Go for it! Consider this your permission slip.

Day 23

MORNING ROUTINE

1. Avoid turning on your phone until you've completed your morning routine.

2. Three Modified Sun Salutations.

3. Five or ten minutes of exercise. If you've been exercising five minutes, extend it to ten minutes. If this is your ONLY exercise of the day, can you extend it to 20 minutes?

4. Five minutes of meditation.

5. Connect with your bigger vision. What are a few of your grandest dreams?

6. Make a list of important things you want or need to do today. Check them off as you accomplish them. Reminding yourself throughout the day by looking at your list will keep you focused. Don't let the minor requests made of you supersede the important things you need to get done. Minimize distractions and get the things done that move your life forward, every day!

7. How do you want to show up in the world?

8. What are you blessed to do?

9. Positive Journaling.

10. Write down your affirmation(s).

EVENING ROUTINE

1. What are you grateful for?

2. Celebrate your accomplishments.

3. How would you rate today and why?

4. What are you excited about/looking forward to tomorrow?

Day 24

MORNING ROUTINE

1. Avoid turning on your phone until you've completed your morning routine.

2. Three Modified Sun Salutations.

3. Ten to twenty minutes of exercise.

4. Five minutes of meditation. Can you extend it to ten minutes?

5. Connect with your bigger vision. What are a few of your grandest dreams? What is the next step or the first step needed to bring this vision to reality? Write it down. Can you make even a small amount of progress towards accomplishing this step today? Maybe it's as simple as ordering a book on the topic? Something that moves you forward is progress. Onward!

6. List of important things to get done today.

7. How do you want to show up in the world?

8. What are you blessed to do?

9. Positive Journaling.

10. Write down your affirmation(s).

EVENING ROUTINE

1. What are you grateful for?

2. Celebrate your accomplishments.

3. How would you rate today and why?

4. What are you excited about/looking forward to tomorrow?

Day 25

MORNING ROUTINE

1. Avoid turning on your phone until you've completed your morning routine.

2. Three Modified Sun Salutations.

3. Ten to twenty minutes of exercise.

4. Five to ten minutes of meditation.

5. Connect with your bigger vision. What are a few of your grandest dreams? What is the next step needed to bring this vision to reality? Take action today! No matter how small or grand, just do something that moves you toward this bigger vision.

6. List of important things to get done today.

7. How do you want to show up in the world?

8. What are you blessed to do?

9. Positive Journaling.

10. Write down your affirmation(s).

EVENING ROUTINE

1. What are you grateful for?

2. Celebrate your accomplishments.

3. How would you rate today and why?

4. What are you excited about/looking forward to tomorrow?

Day 26

MORNING ROUTINE

1. Avoid turning on your phone until you've completed your morning routine.

2. Three Modified Sun Salutations.

3. Ten to twenty minutes of exercise.

4. Five to ten minutes of meditation.

5. Connect with your bigger vision. What are a few of your grandest dreams? What is the next step needed to bring this vision to reality? Take action today!

6. List of important things to get done today. As you make your daily list, what is the ONE thing you

could do that would have the most meaningful impact? What one thing would advance your life more than any other? Take action on this as early in the day as possible.

7. How do you want to show up in the world?

8. What are you blessed to do?

9. Positive Journaling.

10. Write down your affirmation(s).

EVENING ROUTINE

1. What are you grateful for?

2. Celebrate your accomplishments.

3. How would you rate today and why?

4. What are you excited about/looking forward to tomorrow?

Day 27

Repeat Day 26. Tell one person you appreciate them. Show them. Maybe it's a note card, a phone call, a text message or a shout-out on social media. Do something nice for them and let them know they make a difference in your life.

Day 28

Repeat Day 26. Think back to Day 1. What changes do you notice? Do you feel more energetic? More grounded from the meditation and practice of being grateful? Are you any happier? Are your days filled more with things and people that add value to your day and less with the things and people that add stress to your life?

Day 29

Repeat Day 26. Share your experience. Tell a friend about your transformation. Post to social media. Encourage a friend to take the 30-Day Challenge.

Day 30

Make it your own. What parts of the daily routine worked best for you? Create your own daily practice and build it using Word or Adobe Illustrator, etc. so you can print it out. Print several copies, front and back, then take it to a print shop to have it made into your own personal daily journal. Having your journal with you makes it easy to stick to your daily routine and creates a habit which will elevate your life!

Thank you for taking the challenge and I hope that you benefited from it as much as I have. It's been life changing for me and I hope you can say the same!

Gratitude

There are a seemingly endless number of people I am grateful to for helping make my dream of writing a book come true. Thank you to the many people who read the various drafts and provided feedback on the writing and the cover design. I am incredible lucky to have so many friends who have been willing to help me finish this endeavor.

Early on, Stacie Rowland read my first draft and gave me some amazing feedback which caused me to completely rearrange my book and in doing so, the book became much better. When I thought I was finished, I asked my good friend Rose Feliciano to read my book and it came back to me with more edits, comments, questions, and requests for clarification than I would have thought possible. However, as I worked my way through them it quickly became very clear that nearly every point Rose made was spot on and my book was infinitely better for her edit. Rose, I am so grateful for your contribution!

I am especially grateful to Patty Pacelli and Pacelli Publishing for editing and preparing my book to publish through CreateSpace. We live in a world where authors can more easily than ever get their stories out to readers and for that I am very thankful. Without Patty's help, I'm confident I'd still be trying to figure out the process.

The cover was a collaboration of my social media friends and what began as a cover that I thought looked pretty cool became a cover I am extremely proud of. Thank you to the hundreds of friends who provided feedback. Ben Wobker and Kathleen McMahon made some significant contributions – thanks! The heavy lifting came from my friend Dave Masuda. Dave, thank you so much for creating a cover which represents my book; one I will be able to look at for the rest of my life and feel incredibly proud!

I feel very fortunate to have met Kelsey Montgomery and to learn her story. Kelsey, I am honored that you agreed to write the foreword for my book!

Thank you to all my friends who contributed their stories to my book. I am forever honored to have been able to work with you. Your stories help make my words "more than mere words." Thank you, Jennifer MacNiven for creating the video on Sun Salutations for the 30-Day Challenge chapter!

I truly believe this book would never have been more than a someday fantasy if not for my dear friend Allison Walsh. Allison, I cannot adequately express how much respect and admiration I have for you. Thank you for knowing me and understanding me as you do and recommending THREE books that each had an enormous impact on me. That truly was the impetus for me to stop living small and share my story with the world. I am forever grateful for you, friend!

Thank you to the people who've been my teachers along my path of personal growth; Tony Robbins, Brendon Burchard, Hal Elrod, Jon Bergoff, Gay Hendricks, Oprah, Jack Canfield, and Liz Gilbert. I've always believed that most people will never know the extent to which they've impacted other people's lives. Thank you from the bottom of my heart for all you've done for me.

I am grateful for SheAh and Amy, the coaches I worked with one to one who really helped me shift my mindset and move beyond my limiting beliefs. If you'd like to connect with either of them, here is their contact information.

- SheAh Prince Eternal, Personal Life Coach. SheahPrinceEternal.com

- Amy Yamada, Business Mentor for Coaches & Service-Based Entrepreneurs AmyYamada.com

I've been very fortunate to be part of Team In Training for over seventeen years. I'm grateful for all the athletes I've had the privilege of coaching and getting to know. I've been blessed to work closely with some outstanding coaches over the years. Thanks Wade Praeger, Ande Edlund, Cathy McNair, and Gurujan Dourson! I am especially grateful that I've had the honor to attend Dave Scott's Level I & II Team In Training Coaching Certification Courses. Dave, I've learned an incredible amount of triathlon knowledge from you directly as well as through your writings and videos. Thank You! GO TEAM!

Finally, I am grateful for my family and my friends. I am largely the person I am because of my awesome mother. Thanks Mom! While I was in the middle of writing this book, I was in the wedding of one of my best friends, Dustin Hawkins. That weekend I had the great fortune to connect with some dear friends I grew up with - Corey Beck, Steve Wesch, Jason Dill, and Chad Hawkins. While they did not know it at the time, we had some intense conversations that changed my perspective on what I was capable of. It was after that weekend that I really began to believe I could and should not only write this book but put it out for the world to read. Thanks guys! There is no person I am more grateful for than my wife, Janine. You mean the world to me!

I want to leave you with a couple of questions I first heard in one of Hal Elrod's podcasts with Jon Bergoff, "What could your life look like, such that it would cause you to live fully alive and achieve everything you wanted? Who do you need to become in order to live into this vision of yourself and your life?"

Made in the USA
Lexington, KY
25 March 2017